BUILD YOUR OWN

BIRDHOUSES

AND FEEDERS

BUILD YOUR OWN
BIRDHOUSES
AND FEEDERS

FROM SIMPLE, NATURAL DESIGNS TO SPECTACULAR,
CUSTOMIZED HOUSES AND FEEDERS

JOHN PERKINS

FIREFLY BOOKS

A FIREFLY BOOK

Published by Firefly Books Ltd. 1997

Sixth printing, 2011

U.S. Cataloguing-in-Publication Data

Perkins, John

Build your own birdhouses : from classic, simple designs to spectacular customized houses and feeders / John Perkins. – 1st ed.

Originally published: Chartwell Books, 1997.

[144] p. : col. Ill. ; cm.

Includes index.

Summary : Over 25 detailed plans and instructions to building birdhouses of all kinds, and information about attracting birds.

ISBN-13: 978-1-55209-135-7   ISBN-10: 1-55209-135-X

1. Birdhouses — Design and construction. 2. Bird watching   I Title

728.927   –dc21   2000   CIP

Canadian Cataloguing in Publication Data

Perkins, John, 1818

Build your own birdhouses

Includes index

ISBN-13: 978-1-55209-135-7   ISBN-10: 1-55209-135-X

1. Birdhouses – Design and contruction.

2. Bird feeders – Design and construction. I. Title.

QL 676.5.P427 1997 690'8927 C97-930160-2

Published in the United States by
Firefly Books (U.S) Inc.
P.O. Box 1338, Ellicott Station
Buffalo, New York 14205

Published in Canada by
Firefly Books Ltd.
66 Leek Crescent
Richmond Hill, Ontario L4B 1H1

This book was designed and produced by
Quintet Publishing Limited
6 Blundell Street
London N7 9BH

Typeset in Great Britain by
Central Southern Typesetters, Eastbourne
Manufactured in Bath, England by
by DP Graphics
Printed in Singapore by
Star Standard Industries (Pte.) Ltd.

Designer: Heather Blagden
Project Editor: Diana Steedman
Photographers: Keith Waterton, John Melville
Technical Illustrator: David J. Scammell
Step-by-step illustrations:
Hardlines, Charlbury, Oxford
Creative Director: Richard Dewing
Publisher: Oliver Salzmann

Contents

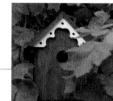

INTRODUCTION

THERE ARE TWO GOOD REASONS FOR ENCOURAGING BIRDS TO FEED IN YOUR GARDEN. ONE IS TO HELP COUNTERACT THE EFFECT THAT MODERN URBANIZATION HAS HAD ON THEIR NATURAL HABITATS AND FEEDING HABITS, IN A SMALL WAY REDRESSING THE BALANCE SO TO SPEAK. THE SECOND IS PURELY SELFISH, AND EMBRACES THE ENJOYMENT, PLEASURE AND RELAXATION THAT WATCHING THEIR COLORFUL RITUALS, DISPLAYS, AND ANTICS CAN BRING TO THE KEEN BIRDER, GARDENER, OR HOUSEHOLDER ALIKE.

BUT, TO ENCOURAGE BIRDS INTO YOUR GARDEN, YOU MUST OFFER THEM SOMETHING IN RETURN, THEIR MOST OBVIOUS NEEDS BEING FOOD AND WATER. IF YOU CAN ALSO PROVIDE SOMEWHERE SAFE FOR THEM TO RAISE THEIR YOUNG OR SHELTER WHEN THE WEATHER'S BAD, THEN THEY IN TURN WILL LEARN TO FEEL SAFE IN YOUR GARDEN

THIS BOOK IS INTENDED FOR THOSE PRACTICAL PEOPLE WHO ENJOY CREATING SOME-THING JUST A LITTLE DIFFERENT: FEEDERS, BIRD TABLES, AND NESTING BOXES THAT WILL HELP TO INTRODUCE YOU TO A NEW AND WORTHWHILE INTEREST, WHILE AT THE SAME TIME INVOLVING YOU IN A FASCINATING AND REWARDING PASTIME.

THE PROJECTS RANGE FROM BASIC AND SIMPLE FEEDERS TO DECORATIVE AND MORE ORNATE BIRDHOUSES. EACH IS DESIGNED TO ENHANCE YOUR GARDEN OR YARD, EACH ANIMATED BY THE BIRDS' NATURAL ABILITY TO FLY.

ENCOURAGING BIRDS

One of the most natural ways of encouraging birds into your garden is to stock it with plants, shrubs, and trees that offer a natural variety of foods and habitats – plants, trees, and shrubs that provide grubs and insects, seeds, and berries; trees and shrubs that will also provide roosting sites and perches, nesting materials and nesting sites.

If you are in the process of planning or landscaping your garden or yard, now is the time to consider planning it to attract and encourage birds. You can do this by incorporating areas of uncut grass and wild flowers, broken up with small trees and shrubs, and by avoiding cutting down any indigenous trees or large shrubs that are likely to already have their dependent local bird population. Do take care to introduce new trees and shrubs that will continue to support local bird populations and further encourage them to remain and expand.

Some species of plants, shrubs, and trees are particular favorites of certain birds. Hawthorn, hemlock, and mulberry, plum and juniper will encourage Blue jays, while elderberry, honeysuckle, sycamore, and willow are attractive to house finches and other small birds. Honeysuckle, Virginia creeper, and elderberry are also firm favorites of the mockingbird, along with crabapple, American bittersweet and cotoneaster.

Do remember, though, that encouraging birds into your garden and gardening for the joy of gardening don't always go hand in hand. The use of pesticides, plant hormones, weedkillers, and preservatives presents a danger to the birds that visit, and in particular to young birds. Passed into the food chain, they can cause enormous harm to present and future generations.

You will also need to ask yourself: Do I really need to keep my grass so short? Areas of longer grass and seeding grasses, wild plants and even weeds, provide a natural diet and habitat for many species.

Vegetable patches are of course of very great interest to many birds, so remember to take extra precautions to protect your fruit and vegetables with nets and cloches.

PREDATORS

The greatest enemy of birds in urban areas is the domestic cat. Cats kill more birds than any other predator. Usually this is not the fault of the owner, although a cat acting as security guard on the vegetable patch of the house next door is quite a deterrent, and licensed to kill! So, if you encourage birds into an urban garden, you must be aware of the dangers that the birds face and take whatever precautions are necessary – even though fencing off areas to separate birds from their chief predators is difficult, and measures such as anti-cat fencing are expensive.

You should also try to deter other predators and competitors (both food and nesting sites are sought-after commodities), such as raccoons and squirrels. Metal posts, especially if well greased, will help to foil attempts to climb them, and a false entrance hole mounted in front of the true hole will limit how far an animal will be able to reach into the box, but will not deter birds from nesting. Squirrels in particular tend to gnaw at the wood surrounding an entrance hole to enlarge it. This can be prevented by fitting a thin, circular, aluminum plate around the hole.

Other measures should also be considered, such as providing adequate trees and bushes or perches for use as lookout posts, and having clear views around feeders, tables, and nesting boxes. Dense ground cover such as shrubs and brush a few yards away from the table or feeder will provide a safe haven where smaller birds can escape the attention of hawks and other birds of prey.

WATER

A constant source of fresh water is essential, both for drinking and bathing. Streams, shallow pools, and even puddles will attract a wide variety of birds and often presents one of the rare occasions when a number of different species will be seen close to each other.

But the water source must always be fresh: a running stream or spring, trickling over a shallow gravel bed, is ideal if not always realistic.

For those with humbler back yards, but a little imagination and innovation, water can still be introduced in an attractive way. Flowing over stepped pools aided by a pumped and filtered recirculating system, water can be used to enhance a garden and provide an area attractive to birds, in a way that is controllable both during the summer months when water may need to be conserved, and most importantly for birds – for short periods during the colder months. In winter, even if the system is activated only when the temperature reaches its higher levels during the day, birds will soon recognize that a regular source of unfrozen water is available and become regular visitors.

Bird baths and water bowls can provide an attractive addition to the garden, but they must be regularly cleaned out and refilled with fresh water, especially in areas where

LEFT *HUMMING-BIRD AT A WATER SUPPLIER. FRESH WATER IS ESSENTIAL TO BIRDS.*

ABOVE *CONSIDER THE SITE FOR YOUR FEEDER. YOU WILL WANT TO VIEW IT WITH EASE ALL YEAR ROUND.*

RIGHT *AN EASTERN BLUEBIRD, WITH BEAUTIFUL SKY BLUE PLUMAGE.*

rainfall is spasmodic or particularly seasonal. Ideally, they should be emptied and refilled daily, especially if well used, as birds do tend to foul them.

THE DOWNSIDE

Of course there is a downside to having birds visit your garden. Birds do make a mess, particularly on hard paved areas. Therefore do consider this when siting bird tables, feeders, roosts, and nesting boxes, preferably having plants or grass around and beneath them.

Do also give a little thought for your neighbors, and don't site feeders, tables, and nest boxes where they can cause a nuisance to them or to passers-by (you may end up getting the dry-cleaner's account).

GARDEN BIRDS

Of course not all birds will be encouraged to nest in your garden, many species being far too timid to risk venturing so close to human habitats. Also, many birds have nesting habits incompatible with the type of birdhouse generally considered desirable for the urban garden. However there are some 80 to 90 permanent and occasional cavity-nesting species in North America alone, many of which are commonly found nesting in urban gardens.

Before copying, adapting, or designing your first birdhouse, do take time to study the birds that already visit your garden. Encourage them by using a feeder or feeding table and get into the habit of documenting the regularity of their visits and their feeding habits. Experiment by putting out different types of food to see which foods attract which birds. Keep a record of your observations through each changing season. Take time to research into their natural habitats, rituals, and routines, so you can provide the best alternative habitat for them. In this way you will experience one of the most enjoyable and satisfying of pastimes.

BELOW *AN ADULT BLUE TIT FEEDS ITS YOUNG INSIDE A MAN MADE NEST BOX.*

MAKING WOODEN BIRDHOUSES, TABLES, AND FEEDERS

MANY OF THE PROJECTS IN THE BOOK WILL INVOLVE YOU IN A RANGE OF SIMPLE WOODWORKING SKILLS REQUIRING ONLY THE BASIC TOOLS LIKELY TO BE FOUND IN ANY HOUSEHOLD TOOLKIT. THE REMAINDER MAY REQUIRE A LITTLE MORE SKILL, BUT NOTHING THAT CANNOT BE ATTEMPTED BY THE COMPETENT AMATEUR .

FOR SOME PROJECTS WE HAVE INTRODUCED A FEW FURTHER TOOLS THAT WE THINK MAY HELP IN SIMPLIFYING THE JOB. THESE ARE LISTED WITHIN THE PROJECT.

SAFETY

As for any woodworking project, safety is of prime importance when using both hand and power tools, so heed these tips:

☆ Make sure your tools are in good condition with the cutting edges sharp, handles securely fitted, and guards in place. Do not ignore guards and safety devises, which are designed to help protect as much as possible;

☆ Always work on a rigid work surface, with the work clamped to it or held in a vise;

☆ Make sure that power cables are kept clear of saw blades and other sharp edges and only use power tools in safe conditions;

☆ Protect yourself from the dangers presented by sawdust, chips,and swarf from sawing, routing, and grinding operations;

☆ Always wear eye protection when grinding or drilling metal, as well as a dust mask or respirator when sanding, sawing, or routing with woodworking machinery or power tools;

☆ Woodworking machines and power tools can also emit high sound levels that, without the protection of ear defenders or muffs, can damage your hearing.

HOW BIG?

Different species of birds will tend to have preferences for the size and shape of a nesting cavity, as well as the size of the entrance hole. However, there are no hard and fast rules on size, because natural habitats do not consist of vast numbers of precisely measured cavities. What *can* be achieved, however, is some control over which species can be excluded from certain boxes to help protect the more vulnerable ones from larger predators or the more aggressive species.

Larger boxes can, of course, be filled with packing materials or fitted with a smaller internal box to accommodate a smaller but interesting tenant.

Ranging in size from around 4½ to 6 in. long, most smaller birds can be accommodated in boxes having a floor area of 4 to 5 in. square and heights ranging from 6 to 12 in. In most cases it is important to allow a height of up to or around 6 in. between the floor and the entrance hole. This is to prevent fledglings from falling or climbing too easily out the box, while allowing for a good insulating layer of nesting material. For larger birds such as bluebirds, robins, starlings, and flickers, boxes should be around 6 in. square but can be of similar height.

Woodpeckers are likely to be attracted to nesting boxes in areas where trees are scarce, preferring to enlarge natural cavities as part of their courting ritual. However, you can encourage them further by filling the box with wood chips and shavings, to give them something to excavate. Boxes should again have a floor area of around 4 to 5 in. square.

For smaller species, entrance holes of 1⅛ to 1½ in. are sufficient, although some species prefer open-fronted boxes or, as in the case of swallows, a wider semicircular entrance. Several of the projects in the book have allowed for different entrance configurations and obviously hole diameters can be changed as required.

BELOW *WOODPECKERS QUITE EASILY EXCAVATE THEIR OWN NEST HOLES BUT SOMETIMES THEY WILL CHOOSE A BIRDHOUSE.*

RIGHT *GREGARIOUS PURPLE MARTINS PREFER TO NEST IN COLONY BIRDHOUSES, AND PAINTED GOURDS ARE PARTICULAR FAVORITES.*

making wooden birdhouses, tables, and feeders

FEEDERS AND TABLES

There is a great deal of diversity in the way various species forage and gather food. When making bird tables allow for these variations by providing support for hanging mesh nut feeders, seedcakes, pieces of fruit, and net bags of bacon rind and other tidbits.

Do avoid using uncoated steel nails, hooks, and screws. These will rust in time leaving sharp points on which birds can injure themselves. Round-headed brass screws or copper nails are far better.

Avoid leaving loose loops and lengths of wire, string, and nylon line that can trap or snare a bird.

Birds do tend to be messy eaters, so always create a raised edge to keep the food on the table. Leave gaps in the edging to allow rainwater to run off.

Regularly remove any uneaten scraps from feeders and tables before they rot, and wash the feeder or feeding surfaces with hot soapy water, to prevent harmful fungi and bacteria growing on them.

NESTING BOXES

Nesting boxes must always have a sloping roof with ample overhang along the edges to allow water to clear quickly away from the sides of the box.

Always position nesting boxes away from the prevailing weather and shield the entrance from driving rain. Try to site any box in a sheltered area out of the prevailing weather.

When young birds first leave the nest and start learning to fly, many of them fall to the ground below the nesting box. So do avoid siting the box over hard or dangerous surfaces, and, to keep predators away, fence off the immediate area at least until the young have left the nest.

In case water does find its way into the nest, leave holes in the bottom or floor of the box to allow it to drain, preventing nesting materials from becoming saturated or the nest filling with rainwater.

All nesting boxes must have access for cleaning, either fitted with a hinged or lift-off roof, or constructed in such a way as the box can be easily separated or lifted off of the floor or base.

Don't be tempted (except with specific birds such as purple martins) to peer into or open the box while there are young birds on the nest. With many species, this can cause the parents to desert their offspring. Never place seed or other food on or around a box in which birds are rearing their young, as this will encourage other birds to land on it, again possibly frightening the breeding pair into leaving the next and abandoning the young.

Nesting boxes should be cleared of old nesting material and washed with hot soapy water at least once a year to rid them of mites. This can be done as soon as the young have left the nest, in the hope that other breeding pairs will use it. Replace some of the nesting material with fresh, and leave a supply of nesting material, such as hair, straw, and wood shavings, close by. You can also leave other materials close to the nest site, such as short lengths of yarn, broken twigs, moss, hair, wool, and wood chips. Leave them in a plastic container hung on its side in a tree or in a bag made from large mesh netting.

MOUNTING TABLES AND BOXES

All bird tables and nesting boxes must be firmly mounted. Insure that tables are set level, and securely attached. Tables and nesting boxes should be at least five feet off the ground to discourage cats and other domestic animals from jumping up onto them.

MOUNTING POSTS

Always insure that the post is strong enough to bear the weight of the birdhouse or table and thick enough to prevent it swaying in the wind. Metal and plastic posts, although arguably less attractive than wooden ones, require less maintenance and cannot be scaled quite as easily by cats and squirrels. If using a wooden post it is worth considering fitting a plastic tube – for example, round- or square-section rainwater pipe – over it.

To deter cats and squirrels from climbing mounting posts, a conical skirt can be fitted around the post, narrow end uppermost. Alternatively the area surrounding the post can be planted with low holly bushes, bush cacti, or similar plants. Fennel or other stiff-stemmed plants, allowed to grow as high as the table, will also act as a deterrent.

Sink your post into the ground at least 18 in. below the surface and surround it with concrete and hard core so that it remains firm. By wrapping plastic around the bottom of the post and lifting it gently out of the hole before the concrete fully cures, a socket can be formed to allow easy removal of the post for maintenance. Place concrete only around the post, not beneath it, otherwise water will not be able to drain from the post hole causing the post to rot.

Concrete post socket

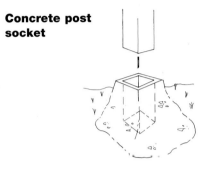

Alternatively a metal, spiked socket, like the ones used for fixing fence posts, can be driven either into firm ground or into concrete. The wooden or metal mounting post can them be clamped into the socket above ground level and easily removed for retreating.

Freestanding posts can be fitted with a trestle-style base, or one weighted with sand or concrete.

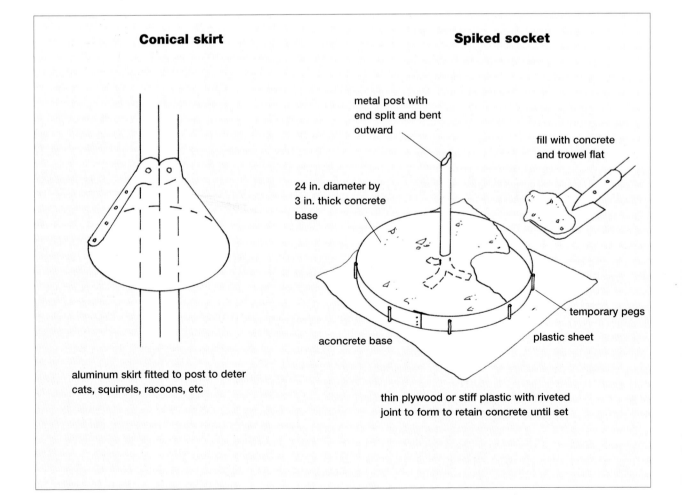

Conical skirt

aluminum skirt fitted to post to deter cats, squirrels, racoons, etc

Spiked socket

metal post with end split and bent outward

fill with concrete and trowel flat

24 in. diameter by 3 in. thick concrete base

aconcrete base

temporary pegs

plastic sheet

thin plywood or stiff plastic with riveted joint to form to retain concrete until set

Freestanding posts

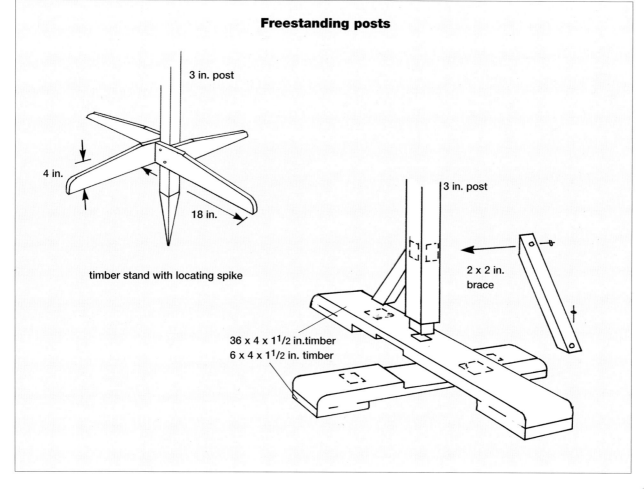

3 in. post

4 in.

18 in.

timber stand with locating spike

3 in. post

2 x 2 in. brace

36 x 4 x 1 1/2 in.timber
6 x 4 x 1 1/2 in. timber

Tools and Techniques

WITH ALL WOODWORKING CAREFUL AND ACCURATE MARKING OUT IS ESSENTIAL TO SAVE TIME AND MATERIALS AND TO ENSURE A SOUND AND PRESENTABLE FINISHED PROJECT. ALWAYS TAKE YOUR TIME OVER MARKING OUT.

MEASURING

You will need a retractable steel tape for measuring and setting out your work. A rigid rule is better for shorter dimensions and can be used as a straight edge for marking out. A long (yard or meter), metal straight edge is also useful for marking out and scoring across panel lines. It can also be used to check that an edge is straight or a panel is flat, by holding it on its edge. Any light seen coming from behind indicates where there are high spots or bowing across the edge or face of the workpiece.

MARKING

Keeping your pencils sharp is essential for accurate marking out but do not sharpen them with your chisels as this will soon take the keenness off the chisel tip. Choose a grade of around HB to 2B – harder ones will indent the wood, making it harder to rub out mistakes, and softer grades produce lines that can be too easily smudged or accidentally wiped off.

When scoring against a square, rule, or straight edge, always make sure you press down hard enough to stop it moving and keep your fingers well away from the edge.

When marking joints and other lines that will be sawn, it is often better to score them with a craft knife or marking gauge rather than using a pencil line. Not only does this leave a fine permanent line, it helps to guide the saw and leaves a sharp edge.

You will also need a try square for marking out at right angles to the edge of the workpiece, particularly when setting out joints and housings. When using the square always hold the stock pressed firmly against the edge of the timber and the blade down onto the wood. Always check that

thero aro no spots of glue or resin on the edge of the wood and that the edge is planed straight, otherwise the line will be out of true.

The try square is also used for checking that the work is square when cutting and assembling.

Steel combination squares can be used for other purposes, such as gauging the depths of mortises, grooves, and so forth, and have an angled stock that can be used for marking out 45-degree angled edges and miters.

A sliding bevel is an adjustable square for marking out angles. Use a plastic protractor to mark the angle on a piece of scrap wood and adjust the blade of the sliding bevel to it, with the stock held against the edge of the wood.

Marking gauges and cutting gauges perform similar tasks when it comes to marking out a line parallel to a straight edge, although a cutting gauge tends to be used more frequently for scribing and scoring a line *across* the grain parallel to the edge. Always check that the edge is straight and square before using a gauge.

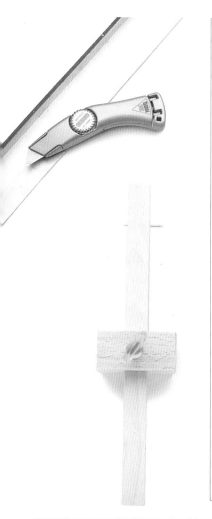

THE ESSENTIAL TOOLKIT

tape measure ✦ steel rule ✦

straight-edge ✦ pencil ✦

craft knife ✦ marking gauge ✦ try square ✦

T-square ✦ jigsaw ✦

handsaws ✦ coping saw ✦ electric drill ✦

drill bits ✦ plane ✦

chisels (¼, ½, ¾ and 1 in.) marking ✦

pin hammer ✦ claw hammer ✦

countersink ✦ nail punch ✦ files ✦

work bench and vice ✦ paint brushes ✦

Extra tools for specific projects are listed
with the projects.

SAWS

There are many different types of saws for cutting wood, and for those new to woodworking the choice can be quite confusing. However, for most projects in this book you will need to be able to make straight and curved lines. The jigsaw is an ideal choice for this, but you will also need a backsaw for cutting rebates and housings.

JIGSAWS

To make life easier and the work a little less strenuous, it is worth investing in a power saw, the most versatile being the electric jigsaw. This has a narrow reciprocating blade that can cut tight curves and circles, as well as straight edges. However, it does not leave very clean or accurate edges, so they will need to be planed or sanded.

Most jigsaws can be used to cut beveled edges with the base plate canted, and for cutting holes and openings by inserting the blade through a predrilled hole. A wide range of blades is available for the jigsaw, including fine- and coarse-cutting types for wood, metal, and plastic, as well as narrow blades for cutting tight curves and fretwork.

For cutting in a straight line, the jigsaw can be run against a straight edge, or fitted with a parallel edge guide. Do not force the blade, or else the teeth will clog with sawdust and it will overheat. Avoid applying sideways pressure as this will bend the blade, leaving a ragged and angled cut. Always start with the base of the saw resting firmly on the material, but let the motor build up to full speed before starting to cut. To prevent the edges of the wood lifting when cutting curves or across the grain, it is worth scoring along the line with a craft knife prior to cutting.

Bandsaw

CIRCULAR SAWS

Portable circular power saws are mainly used for cutting long lengths and large sheet material. However, a table-mounted saw is ideal for ripping and crosscutting large and small pieces and, if fitted with a sliding miter fence, for cut-

ting miters and squaring ends. Some saws can be adapted for cutting rebates, tenons and so on, but do not do this if it means removing the blade guards. Always insure that guards are securely fitted and use a push stick to move the lumber through the blade, keeping your hands well clear.

BAND SAW

Another powered and very useful saw for this type of project is the bandsaw. Capable of cutting both curved and straight edges, most models have a tilting table for cutting miters and bevels.

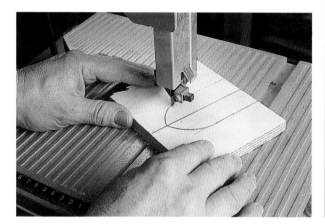

HANDSAWS

Various types of backsaws are available, having a brass or steel rib fitted along the top of the blade to keep it rigid. Those for general small-scale work have about 14 to 18 teeth per inch, the larger number being finer and therefore leaving a neater cut edge. Backsaws are used mainly for cutting joints and across the grain. Always keep the teeth sharp and correctly set (it is best to regularly take it to a saw doctor for sharpening and setting). Cheaper saws tend to be of the hard-tooth throwaway type. These initially have very sharp durable teeth, but once they have become blunt or damaged they cannot be resharpened. However, they do tend to have a fairly long life and are therefore ideal for small projects such as these.

Coping and fretsaws are used for cutting curves and internal cutouts by hand, having a fine blade that turns easily in the cut. For internal cuts, one end is detached from the saw and inserted through a predrilled hole in the waste part of the cutout. The end is then fitted back in the saw for cutting. Always work with a sharp blade set taut and try to avoid twisting it in the cut.

Copingsaw

Jigsaw

Backsaw

Although traditional hand drills and braces are still used, most amateur woodworkers now tend to use power drills. Two types are available: the more powerful mains voltage drills and the safer battery-operated or cordless drills.

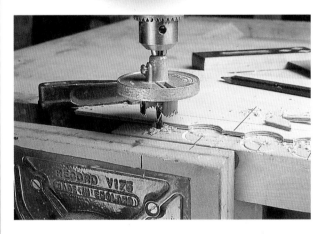

Holesaw

For the projects in this book, a reasonable-quality cordless drill will be quite suitable, especially if it is of the higher-voltage type (9.6 or 12 volt), and has a screwdriving facility.

With the exception of good-quality, high-voltage, cordless drills, larger-diameter bits, such as holesaws and flat (spade) bits, are best used in mains-power drills. Although they can be used in a hand-held drill, it is safer to use them with the drill mounted in a drill press. Always clamp the wood securely, over a piece of scrap material. The scrap both supports the workpiece and prevents the wood breaking out on the back face as the bit or saw breaks through.

Holesaws can also be used to cut semicircular shapes for miniature decorative work such as for the bargeboards of the beach-hut nesting box in this book.

PLANING

Virtually any sawn edge will need planing to finish it straight and square and for this you will need a bench plane. These come in various sizes. The longer the plane, the easier it is to plane a long edge straight. For these projects a smoothing plane or the larger jack plane is best suited. To work correctly and make the job easier, plane irons (blades) must be kept sharp (honed). This you can do on an oil or diamond stone, but do use a honing roller guide, as you can easily lose the angle of the cutting edge or round it over. Hand planes are used for two purposes: for reducing the size of a

piece of wood and for flattening and smoothing the surface. For either purpose take only thin shavings in order not to waste effort or wood.

Special-purpose planes include rabbet and plow planes for cutting rebates and grooves. These are quite expensive items and do need a measure of skill to use. Short rebates and grooves can be cut by sawing along the lines with a backsaw and removing any remaining waste with a sharp chisel. Rebates and grooves can also be cut with a power saw or table saw (see **Saws**) or most effectively with an electric router.

SCREWDRIVERS

Always use a screwdriver of the correct size and width to suit the screw size, otherwise you will damage the head, making it difficult to drive and, if necessary, to remove. Take care not to raise a burr on the screw head as these can be extremely sharp and may cause injury to anyone using or handling the finished product. Cross-head screws are particularly easy to use especially if you are inserting them with an electric screwdriver. Again, you will need a range of different-sized cross-head screwdrivers or hexagonal shank bits for a power screwdriver.

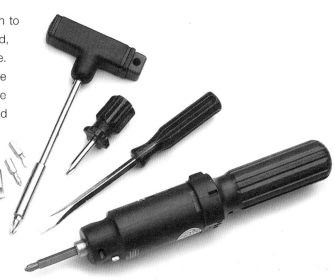

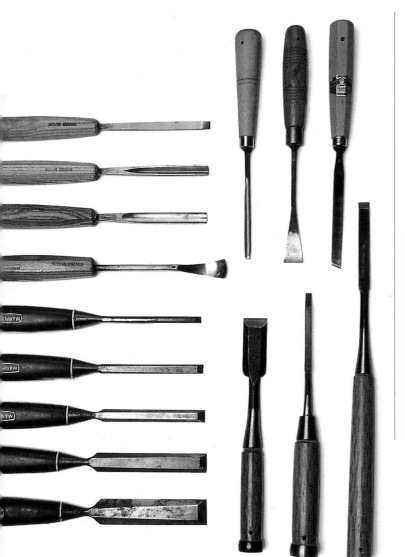

You will need several chisels, ideally ¼, ⅜, ½ and 1 in. wide. While firmer chisels (with a square edge) are stronger, bevel-edge chisels have some advantage when trimming into tight corners or pockets. Modern chisels with shatterproof plastic handles can be used for most cutting operations using hand pressure only, or driven with a wooden mallet. Do not use a hammer on a chisel handle (wood or plastic), as it will split it or raise sharp edges. When using a chisel, always keep both hands behind the cutting edge.

TOOL TIPS

As with all cutting-edge tools, chisels must be

kept sharp to make the job easier and safer.

Sharp tools need far less

force to achieve results than blunt ones,

making them easier to control and less likely

to catch the user unawares.

HAMMERS

You will need two types of hammer: a general-duty claw hammer for knocking in and taking out large nails, and a pin hammer for panel pins, molding pins and brads. You will also need a couple of nail punches, one for large nails and a narrow one for panel and molding pins.

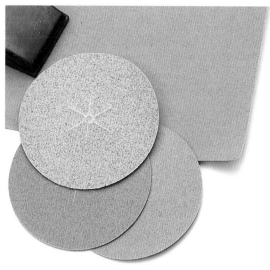

RASPS, FILES, AND SANDERS

For the more awkward places and narrow edges, it is generally easier to finish the surface by hand, using a rasp, file, or abrasive paper.

Rasps are used to remove wood fast and leave a fairly coarse finish. Take care when using them across the grain, particularly on plywood edges, as they tend to tear the grain, leaving a fairly jagged edge. Always work with or at a slight angle to the grain.

Files give a finer cut and are mainly used to smooth and add fine detail, but tend to clog when working wood. Keep a wire brush handy for cleaning them.

Modern abrasive papers such as those with silicon and aluminum oxides, have a far longer life than traditional sand and glasspapers. They also cut better and clog less. For most sanding operations the abrasive paper should be used with a cork or wooden backing block, either flat or curved, to match the surface contour you are sanding. Round or irregular internal surfaces can be sanded using abrasive paper wound round a piece of dowel.

Much of the tediousness of sanding can be avoided by using an electric sander, of which there are various types. The most commonly used sanders for surface finishing are orbital sanders. Denoted as ½ or ⅓ sheet sanders or ¼ sheet palm sanders, these have a flat base that operates with a slight oscillating motion following an oval orbit. These are most suited to fine sanding and flatting between coats of paint or varnish.

Sanding disks are generally fitted to a rubber backing pad held in an electric drill. This rotates at the drill speed. In use, the disk can easily leave deep score marks. Random-orbit sanders use an eccentric drive to prevent the orbits coinciding, leaving an almost perfect finish. With coarse and fine disks, random-orbit sanders can be used to remove material as well as to bring the surface to a fine, smooth finish.

Belt sanders remove wood very quickly, and are generally used for shaping and finishing sawn or rough wood. However, fitted with a sanding table and adjustable fence, they are ideal for squaring edges or shaping small pieces.

WORKBENCH AND VISE

A rigid workbench fitted with a reasonable-sized vise is essential for ease, convenience, and safety when working. It can either be a fixed bench – although this calls for somewhere permanent to keep it – or a folding portable bench that can be used anywhere. The vise must be of a quality that will insure that materials and workpieces are held securely, and should be fitted with wooden faces to prevent damage to the work.

ELECTRIC ROUTERS

Electric routers are ideal for squaring and shaping edges, both for jointing and decorative purposes, as well as for trimming and cutting slots and grooves. Fitted with a trammel point, routers can be used to cut precise circles and arcs.

Because the cutter is held at a precise right angle to the surface of the wood, and the cutter action is against the cut edge rather than across it, routers leave square clean edges that require little cleaning up or planing.

For cutting circles the router is swung around a trammel point pressed into the surface of the work. The point is fitted either on a rod clamped to the base of the router, or to a false base plate screwed beneath the router. Always swing the router against the rotation of the cutter (i.e. clockwise on internal cuts, counterclockwise on external cuts),

and take care to keep the cable safely out of the way. When you are cutting completely through the work, always mount it on a piece of waste material to allow the cutter to cut deeper than the thickness of the wood.

Large-diameter circles can be cut with a trammel rod. The rod has a center pin fitted at

For pitched roofs and angled walls it is necessary to plane an accurate bevel along the edge of the panel. To do this first set out the angle on either end of the wood. Connect the bottom of the angles with a line drawn or scored across the face of the panel. Secure the panel in the vise and hold the plane at approximately the bevel angle. Taking only fine shavings, plane away the wood down to the line, leaving a flat face from the apex of the edge to the line.

TURNING

Roof finials can be easily turned on a basic lathe. Plane a piece of wood ¼ to ½ in. larger in section than the finished diameter. Plane the wood to a hexagonal section and fit it between the lathe centers. Roughly turn the wood, cutting

one end and is held in the side fence clamp, allowing the distance between the center point and the cutter to be adjusted to the circle diameter.

Small-diameter circles can be cut with a false base fitted to the router, drilled to take a pin. The pin is pressed into the surface at the center point of the circle and the router swung about it. The diameter of the circle is measured from the pin to the edge of the cutter. Different diameters can be accommodated by drilling equally spaced holes across the false base. Rings can also be cut in this way, but do insure that the ring as well as the waste is pinned or glued to a cutting board to allow the cutter to cut fully through the material.

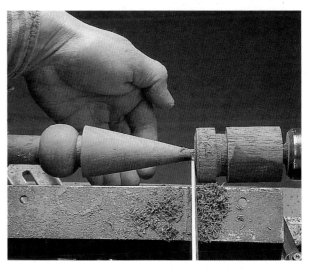

with a suitable turning tool, until it is completely round. Mark out with a pencil the length and position of each recess, taper and ridge. Rough out the shape with a turning gouge, re-marking each part as necessary. Finish the surface smooth with a flat turning chisel – although this could be difficult and tricky if you're a novice – before finishing with abrasive paper.

Carefully remove the finial from the lathe using a parting tool or saw.

CUTTING REBATES

Rebates for forming right-angled joints can be cut in three ways. The first is by hand, using a handsaw to cut the edge of the rebate on the face and edge. On plywood the first cut can be made on the face but the waste can then be pared away with a chisel. In either case score both lines with a craft knife.

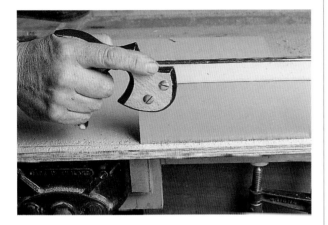

Alternatively, a rebate plane can be used. After marking the width and depth of the rebate, score both lines as before. Holding the plane against the scored lines in turn, adjust the depth stop and side fence. Set the blade to take a fine shaving and plane down from the face to the full rebate depth. Keep the vertical face of the plane firmly against the cut face.

Possibly the easiest method is to use an electric router, fitted either with a special self guiding rebate cutter or a straight bit guided by the side fence supplied with the machine. After carefully setting the final depth of cut on the router's depth gauge, adjust the actual cutting depth to no more than $\frac{1}{8}$ in. Set the full width of the rebate using the side fence adjustment, and cut an initial shallow rebate. Increase the depth of cut by a similar amount and make subsequent cuts until the full depth of the rebate is reached.

Rebates can also be cut using the router freehand, that is without the side fence or cutter guide. When doing this, saw or plane the face of the work flat and hold the router securely, keeping it against the work face. Draw a line to mark the width of the rebate and work in steps until the full depth is reached. Work around the rebate in a clockwise direction (that is against the rotation of the cutter).

GLUING REBATES

Fasten the joint by gluing and pinning the two panels together. Support one side of the joint either in a vise on the bench and wipe off any excess glue before it dries. When dry, plane and/or sand the edge of the joint flush.

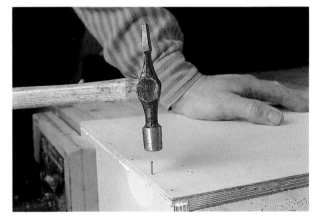

MATERIALS AND FINISHING

As birdhouses will need to survive both wind and rain as well as sunshine, it is worth spending a little extra on materials and finishes that will stand up to the extremes. However, to be sure of their lasting, it is necessary to repair and repaint them at least annually.

One of the best materials for making nesting boxes, bird tables and feeding stations is exterior-grade plywood. Although quite expensive compared with many other materials, it is durable, strong, and has good insulation qualities. Other sheet materials, such as chipboard and MDF (even moisture-resistant grades are not intended for exterior use), should be used only for boxes that will be kept under shelter.

Solid wood is also used, both for constructing the box walls or roofs, and for beads, battens, and blocks for gluing and strengthening joints. These can be either hardwood or softwood, but only durable timbers should be used.

Alternatively, waste and scrap wood can be used, but do beware of nails and staples that can cause injury to anyone handling it and to the sharp cutting edges of hand tools, power tools and woodworking machines.

Wood is usually bought as either sawn lumber (straight

from the mill saws) or planed, having been planed smooth on each face with the edges and faces square to each other. Although more expensive, the latter requires less preparation and is easier to handle and use. Planed surfaces require less sanding and will take paint fiishes far better.

Exterior plywood can be cut and worked with normal wood-working tools, but large sheets (96 x 48 in.) can be heavy and difficult to handle. Smaller-cut sheets are easier to handle and available in either set sizes or cut to order, but will generally be more expensive. However, as most of the projects in this book use a comparatively small amount of material, buying part-sheets of plywood and other materials will be the most convenient and economical way. When buying plywood for this type of project, select material that is made up of many equal-thickness veneers rather than those with a thick center core. Most of the birdhouses and feeders shown in this book are made from exterior-grade B birch plywood. One of the benefits of this is that its light color and close-grained surface will take paint and wood stains well, without affecting the color.

GLUE AND FASTENINGS

Many of the projects in the book have glued and pinned joints, either rebated or reinforced with glued battens or blocks. Only exterior-grade adhesives should be used, either of PVA or epoxy resin formulation. Boat-building adhesives are certainly worth considering, in particular those with gap-filling properties. Although expensive, two-part resin adhesives are extremely durable and have excellent adhesion qualities with most woods and wooden sheet materials.

Rusting can cause steel fastenings such as screws, nails, and pins to work loose fairly quickly, so consider using brass copper, stainless steel, aluminum or monometal fastenings. If you're using steel pins, punch the heads below the surface. This helps to prevent them working proud with the risk of injuring birds or anyone handling the nesting box or feeder. Abrasions caused by rusty fastenings can become septic.

FILLING AND SEALING

Before painting, any defects in the surface of the wood, sunken nail- and screw-head holes, and other gaps should be filled to prevent water lodging in them. For this purpose use a two-part filler such as that used for car body work. Sand the surface well, after it has set, and dust off the residue.

To reduce the ingress of moisture, wood surfaces can be sealed with exterior UPVA adhesive thinned with water or thin resin. For a more long-lasting finish, a thin sheathing of resin and fiberglass mat can be applied. The surface can then be sanded and painted as before.

PAINT AND VARNISHES

As the long-term effects of treating birdhouses, tables and feeders with wood preservatives is not fully known, it is advisable to minimize the risk and use those preservatives that are known to be less toxic. Also, treat only the outside of the box, as young birds are likely to peck and scratch at the inside. Water-based preservatives are claimed to be safer, as are water-based paint finishes.

The finish used on most of the projects is masonry paint with a fine-textured finish. When buying the paint look out for small color-match sample tins, rather than buying a large amount. Water-based, wood-shade and colored varnishes can also be used, but again not on the inside.

Bird house projects

from the Wild West

to an urban landscape

- a host of houses for nesting birds

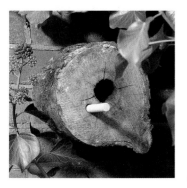

HOLLOW LOGS

SECTIONS CUT FROM HOLLOW BRANCHES OR TREE TRUNKS ARE IDEAL FOR MAKING NATURAL BIRDHOUSES, BY FITTING A PLYWOOD PLATE OVER ONE OR BOTH ENDS OF THE HOLE THEY CAN BE HUNG ON A WALL OR SECURED TO THE TRUNK OR BETWEEN THE BRANCHES OF A TREE. THE PLYWOOD FRONT CAN BE CUT COMPLETE WITH THE ENTRANCE HOLE, OR CUT STRAIGHT ACROSS TO FORM AN OPEN-FRONTED BOX. AN ALTERNATIVE TO USING A HOLLOW LOG IS TO CUT THE CENTER OUT OF A SOLID ONE, REBATE THE ENDS AND FIT END PLATES AS BEFORE. SUITABLE FOR ALL CAVITY-NESTING BIRDS, DEPENDING ON THE INTERNAL SIZE AND ENTRANCE CONFIGURATION OR DIAMETER.

MATERIALS

1 short log 8–14 in. diameter

1 piece of 6 x 6 x ⅜ or ¼ in. plywood

1 piece of 3 x ¼ in. diameter dowel

1 length of stiff wire

screws

OTHER TOOLS

Router and large diameter (¾ in. plus) straight bit

½ in. diameter flat or spade bit

CUTTING THE HOLE

1 Cut both faces of the branch or log with a saw, leaving it flat and reasonably smooth. If required, use a chisel and wooden mallet to enlarge the hole. Work with the grain direction, cutting away thin shavings. If you wish to cut a new hole in a log, use a flat bit or auger to drill a ring of holes. Knock out the center waste and pare the sides with a chisel to finish them smooth.

2 Choose a round container, paint can or similar, that is about an inch larger in diameter than the irregular hole in the log. Place this over the irregular hole and draw round it with a pencil.

3 Fit a large-diameter straight cutter in the electric router.

4 Set the depth of cut to ⅛ in. With the router firmly supported on the timber face and firmly gripped in both hands, cut round the edge of the hole in a clockwise direction. Aim to remove about ¼ in. of wood from the edge at a time, slowly increasing the rebated area up to the line. Having cut around the line,

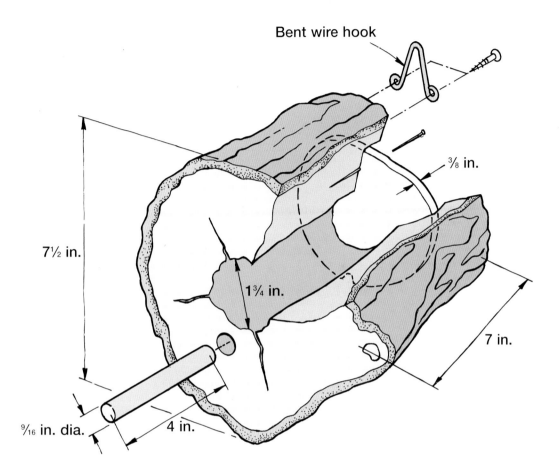

Bent wire hook

7½ in.

3/8 in.

1¾ in.

7 in.

9/16 in. dia.

4 in.

increase the depth of cut and repeat the process until the full ½ in. is completely removed.

5 Alternatively, a sharp chisel can be used, first marking the depth of the hole and cutting from the side before cutting to clear the remaining wood. Use a wooden mallet to drive the chisel.

END PLATES

6 On ⅜ in. plywood, draw around the container used to mark out the rebate. Cut out the circular plate with a jigsaw and trim with a rasp until it is a fairly close fit in the rebate in the log.

7 Use a hole saw to cut the entrance hole when fitting a plate to the front of a hollow log. Drill a small hole or cut a small notch at the bottom of the plate to allow for drainage.

8 If preferred, the outside face of the plate can be painted with masonry paint or water-based stain or varnish, before being fitted.

9 Screw or nail the plate into the rebate.

MOUNTING

10 To enable the log to be hung on a wall or post, bend a piece of stiff wire with a circular twist at each end, and fix it to the back of the log with two wood screws.

FLOWERPOTS

A N ECONOMICAL METHOD OF MAKING NESTING BOXES, SIMPLY BY FITTING A FALSE PLATE TO CLOSE THE OPEN END OF THE POT. THE PLYWOOD FRONT CAN BE CUT COMPLETE WITH THE ENTRANCE HOLE, OR CUT STRAIGHT ACROSS TO FORM AN OPEN-FRONTED BOX. SUITABLE FOR ALL CAVITY-NESTING BIRDS, DEPENDING ON THE OVERALL SIZE OF THE POTS AND ENTRANCE CONFIGURATION OR DIAMETER.

1 Using any size of traditional terracotta flowerpot, measure the inside diameter within the stepped rim of the pot.

2 Set a pair of compasses to that diameter and draw out the circle on ⅜ in. thick solid wood or plywood. Score along the line and cut around it with a jigsaw.

3 Use a masonry bit to drill two holes in opposite sides of the pot rim, and use a larger drill to countersink them.

4 Either cut an entrance hole, the size depending on the pot and the bird species you wish to attract, or cut part of the circle away to produce an open-front birdhouse. At the bottom of the disk cut a small notch across its edge to allow the pot to drain if necessary.

5 Block the drainage hole in the base of the terracotta pot with an epoxy filler plug.

6 Fit the disk in the rim of the pot and insert the two screws.

7 Paint the outside face of the disk with terracotta masonry paint.

MOUNTING

● Use stiff garden wire to make a cradle for hanging the pot in a tree or bush. Alternatively cut a small-diameter wooden disk, slightly larger than the drainage hole in the end of the pot, and drill a hole through its center. Screw the pot onto a wall or wooden surface using a long wood screw and an angled block to tilt the pot downward.

MATERIALS

Terracotta flower pots
6–12 in. diameter
1 piece of 12 x 12 x ⅜ or
¼ in. plywood
Screws
Terracotta paint

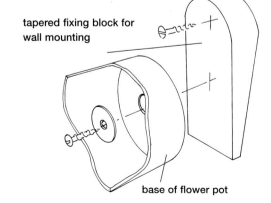

tapered fixing block for wall mounting

base of flower pot

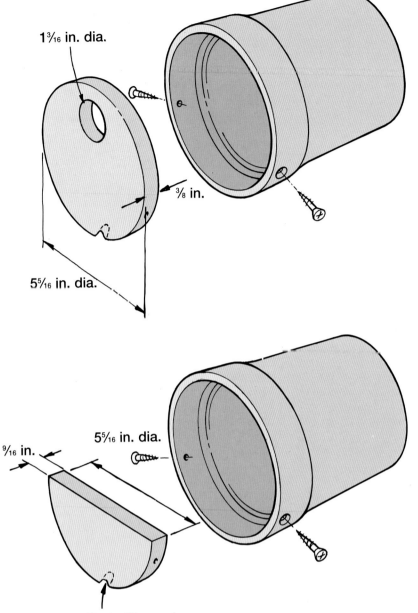

1³⁄₁₆ in. dia.

³⁄₈ in.

5⁵⁄₁₆ in. dia.

5⁵⁄₁₆ in. dia.

⁹⁄₁₆ in.

Drain Channel

TRIANGULAR BOX

THIS MODERN GEOMETRIC DESIGN CAN BE WALL- OR POST-MOUNTED. ITS SIMPLE PULL-OUT FRONT ALLOWS IT TO BE QUICKLY EMPTIED OUT AND CLEANED. IDEAL FOR ALL SMALL BIRDS SUCH AS HOUSE WRENS, CHICKADEES, AND WOODPECKERS. DON'T FORGET TO ADD SOME WOOD CHIPS AND OTHER NESTING MATERIALS TO ENCOURAGE THE CAVITY-NESTERS.

MATERIALS

1 piece of 24 x 24 x ⅜ in. plywood
1 piece of 3 x ⅜ in. diameter dowel
1 piece of 6 x 1 x ⅜ in. timber
1 piece of 12 x 3 x ¾ in. timber
Exterior wood glue
Stain and paint
¾ in. molding pins
Brass hook and eye

BACK AND ROOF

1 Cut the triangular (45:45:90 deg.) back panel and two roof panels from ⅜ in. plywood, scoring across the grain with a craft knife and finishing the edges square with a plane.

2 Plane a bevel of 45 deg. along one short edge of the two roof panels.

3 Glue and pin the two roof panels to the triangular back, leaving a ¼ in. lip along the rear edges.

FRONT

4 Cut the triangular front and rectangular bottom panels from ⅜ in. plywood and plane the edges square. Finish the length of the bottom panel the same dimension as the base of the triangular front. Trim both ends of the bottom to an angle of 45 deg. Glue and pin the two pieces together, with a ⅛ in. overlap to leave a lip along the bottom edge.

5 Drill the entrance hole with a 1–1¼ in. diameter hole saw to suit specific bird species. Cut a 3 in. length of ¼ in. diameter dowel and glue it into a hole drilled beneath the entrance hole.

6 After filling any defects and recessed pin and screw heads with epoxy filler, sand all surfaces smooth. Paint the outer walls, roof, and base with an exterior masonry paint or water-based stain or varnish.

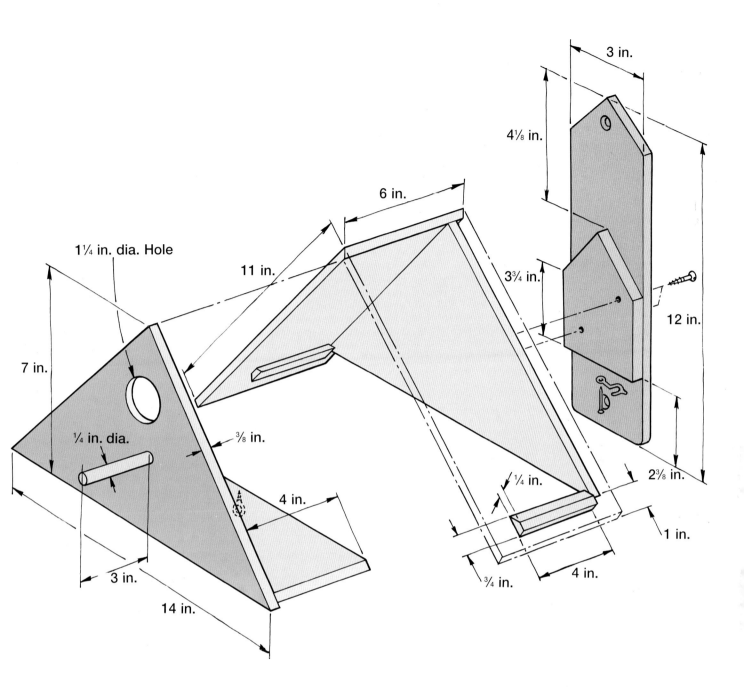

1¼ in. dia. Hole

11 in.

6 in.

3 in.

4⅛ in.

3¾ in.

7 in.

¼ in. dia.

⅜ in.

4 in.

¼ in.

12 in.

2⅜ in.

1 in.

¾ in.

4 in.

3 in.

14 in.

SLIDES

7 Cut a solid batten (8¼ x ¾ x ¼ in.) and plane a 45-deg. angle along one edge. Cut the batten in half, and, with the front of the box in place, glue and pin each piece to the inside face of the roof panels,

checking that the front slides in and out easily. Wipe away any excess glue before leaving to dry.

8 Fit a small brass hook to the bottom edge of the rear panel to locate into a brass eye screwed into the underside of the floor.

MOUNTING

9 Cut the rear mounting bracket and the spacing piece from a piece of 3 x ¾ in. wood and trim one end of both pieces to a 45-deg. apex. Glue and screw the two pieces to the back panel, insuring that the screws do not penetrate into the nesting box.

BASIC BOXES

THESE BASIC NESTING BOXES HAVE A SLOPING ROOF WITH

OVERHANGING AND LIPPED EDGES TO PREVENT RAIN FROM GETTING

IN, AND THEY'RE HINGED FOR EASY CLEANING. EITHER THE ENTRANCE-HOLE OR OPEN-

FRONTED TYPE, MOUNTED ON A POST OR WALL, WILL ATTRACT MOST CAVITY-NESTING BIRDS.

HOWEVER, DON'T BE TEMPTED TO KEEP LOOKING IN AT THE YOUNG BIRDS: YOU MIGHT

FRIGHTEN THE PARENTS AWAY.

WALLS

1 Cut four sides, one each 6 x 7¾ in. and 6 x 9¾ in. and two 5½ x 9¼ in, from ⅜ in. plywood.

2 Mark out on the two side pieces the roof angle. Score across the grain and cut to this angle. Clamp both together in the vise and plane to the same size, leaving the edges square.

3 Mark out the rebate on the vertical inside face of the front and back. These are equal to the thickness of the plywood (⅜ in.) on the inside face of each piece and to a depth of ³⁄₁₆ in.

4 Score across the grain on both pieces, before cutting with a backsaw to the depth on the inside of the line. Pare the plywood veneers away with a chisel to form the rebates.

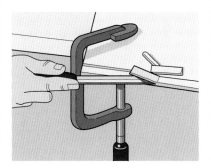

5 Glue and pin the four walls together checking that the bottom edges are flush and that the corners are square.

MATERIALS

1 piece of 30 x 18 x ⅜ in. plywood

1 piece of 12 x 3 x ¾ in. timber

1 piece of 6 x ½ x ½ in. triangular bead

Exterior wood glue

Stain and paint

¾ in. molding pins

1 brass hinge

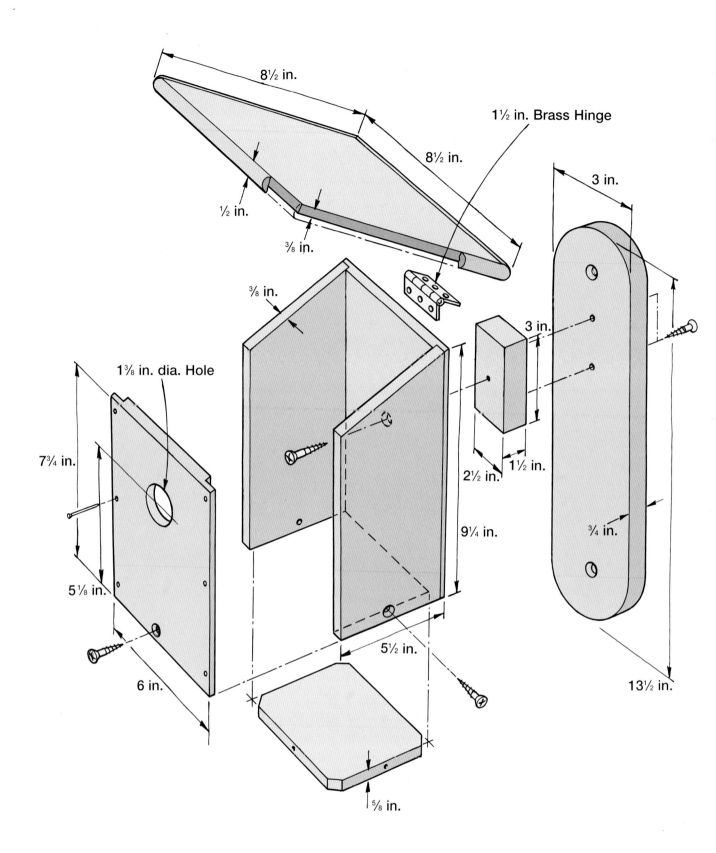

8½ in.

1½ in. Brass Hinge

8½ in.

3 in.

½ in.

⅜ in.

⅜ in.

3 in.

1⅜ in. dia. Hole

7¾ in.

2½ in.

1½ in.

9¼ in.

5⅛ in.

¾ in.

6 in.

5½ in.

13½ in.

⅝ in.

6 When dry, plane the top edge of the front and rear walls to follow the side-wall roof angle.

7 Cut the floor from ⅜ in. plywood, to a push fit inside the walls. Plane the edges square and trim the corners at 45 deg. (for drainage). Drill the four walls and screw the floor in place.

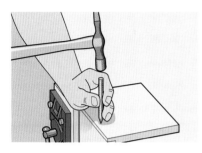

8 Draw a center line down the front face. Cut the entrance hole with a 1–1¼ in. hole saw to suit specific species. Alternatively cut a 1½ in. deep slot across the top of the front panel, finishing at each end in a curve.

9 Cut the 8½ x 8½ in. roof from ⅜ in. plywood and plane the edges square.

10 Cut and miter four lengths of ½ in. half-round bead and glue and pin them to the roof edges.

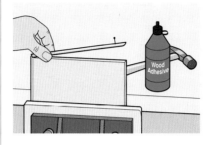

MOUNTING

11 From ¾ in. wood cut a 3 x 13½ in. plate and round each end. Drill and countersink two ³⁄₁₆ in. screw holes at each end. From 1½ in. lumber cut a 3 x 2½ in. block. Screw and glue the block to the back of the box and screw the plate to it.

FINISHING TOUCHES

After filling any defects and recessed pin and screw heads with epoxy filler, sand all surfaces smooth. Paint the outer walls, roof, and base with non-toxic stain or varnish or masonry paint. After painting, screw the lid to the box using a 1½ in. brass hinge.

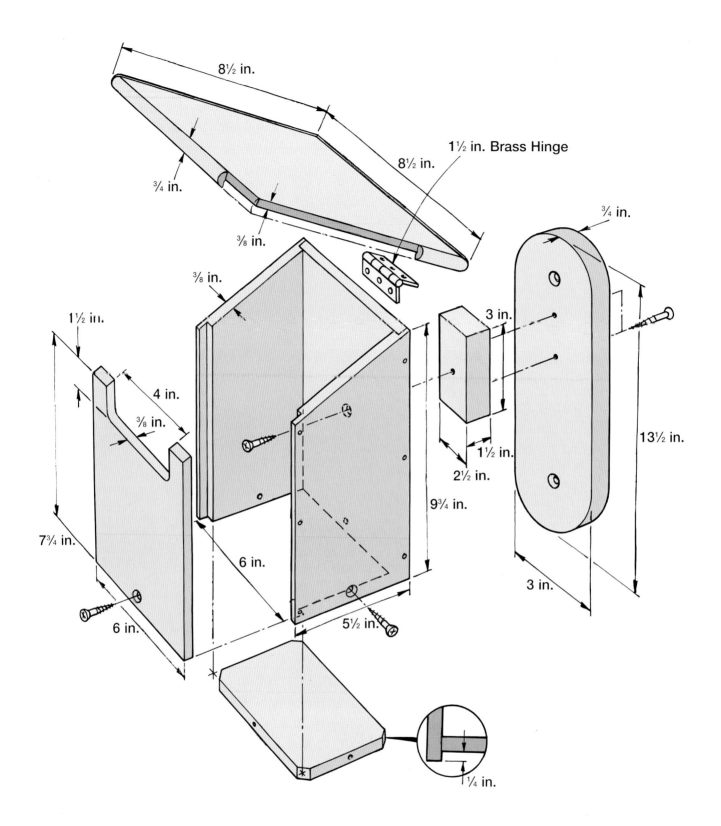

8½ in.

¾ in.

⅜ in.

1½ in. Brass Hinge

8½ in.

¾ in.

⅜ in.

3 in.

1½ in.

1½ in.

4 in.

⅜ in.

13½ in.

2½ in.

7¾ in.

9¾ in.

6 in.

6 in.

5½ in.

3 in.

¼ in.

GARDEN SHED

AN OBVIOUS CHOICE FOR ANY GARDEN, THIS SCALED-DOWN POTTING SHED, COMPLETE WITH ITS GARDEN BENCH, MAKES THE IDEAL NESTING BOX FOR ANY OF THE SMALLER BIRD SPECIES SUCH AS CHICKADEES, HOUSE WRENS, THE TUFTED TITMOUSE, AND WOODPECKERS. CHANGE THE ENTRANCE HOLE DIAMETER OR CUT DOWN THE DOOR TO ATTRACT OTHER BIRDS SUCH AS ROBINS AND SWALLOWS.

MATERIALS

1 piece of 18 x 18 x ¼ in. plywood

1 piece of 8 x ¼ in. diameter dowel

1 piece of 10 x ¼ in. timber

1 piece of 8 x 6 x ½ in. plywood

Exterior wood glue

Stain and paint

¾ in. molding pins

WALLS

1 Cut two 4 x 7¾ in. and two 3½ x 7¾ in. pieces from ¼ in. plywood. Clamp each pair in turn in the vise and plane to the same size, leaving the edges square.

2 Draw out on the larger two, the 45-deg. roof pitch. Score across the grain and cut to this angle. Plane a 45-deg. chamfer along the top edges of the smaller side walls.

3 Mark out the rebate on the vertical panels of the front and back. This is equal to the thickness of the plywood (¼ in.) on the inside face of each piece and to the depth of three veneers (layers) on the edges.

4 Score across the grain on both pieces, before cutting with a backsaw to the depth of three veneers. Pare the veneers away with a chisel to form the rebates.

5 Carefully mark out the window and door openings, and score across the grain where necessary. Make the openings using a backsaw to cut down the grain and a coping saw to cut across. Finish the edges with a file and abrasive paper, leaving a straight edge.

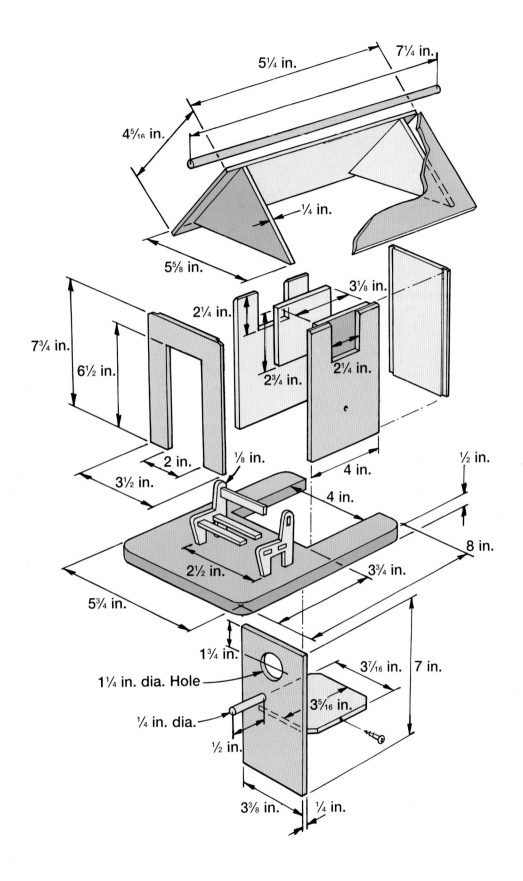

5¼ in.

7¼ in.

4⁵⁄₁₆ in.

¼ in.

5⅝ in.

3⅛ in.

2¼ in.

7¾ in.

6½ in.

2¾ in.

2¼ in.

2 in.

⅛ in.

4 in.

3½ in.

½ in.

4 in.

8 in.

2½ in.

3¾ in.

5¾ in.

1¾ in.

1¼ in. dia. Hole

3⁷⁄₁₆ in.

7 in.

3⁵⁄₁₆ in.

¼ in. dia.

½ in.

3⅜ in.

¼ in.

6 Glue and pin the sides together and check that the corners are square. When dry, plane or sand the edges flush.

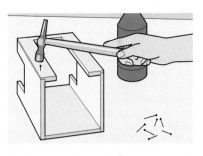

ROOF

7 Cut the roof panels to size and plane the edges square. Mark out and cut the 45 deg. triangular end pieces to size and plane the edges square. Glue and pin the panels together to form the pitched roof. Cut a ¼ in. diameter length of dowel 2 in. longer than the roof, and glue it in the 90-deg. angle left along the apex of the roof.

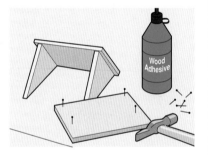

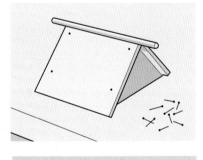

BASE

8 Mark out the outside edges of the 8 x 5¾ in. base and the corner radius. Score across the grain and around the corner radius. Cut the base out with a jigsaw and finish by planing the straight edges and sanding the corners smooth with a sanding block and abrasive paper.

9 Draw the cutout for the shed on the base and score across the grain. Cut the openings using a backsaw to cut down the grain and a coping saw to cut across. Fit the assembled walls into the cutout, gluing and pinning through the front and side walls.

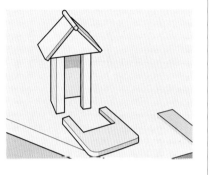

WINDOWS AND DOOR

10 Cut the two window panels, sand smooth and paint black, leaving a glue margin on three sides. Glue the panels to the inside of the side walls and clamp until dry.

11 Cut out the door and floor of the nesting box, and cut the angled corners of the latter. Glue and pin the pieces together allowing adequate depth for the nest (this may vary with the species size), to prevent the young chicks from falling or climbing too easily through the entrance hole, until they are ready to leave the nest.

12 Cut the entrance hole with a hole saw of 1–1¼ in. to suit specific bird species. Cut a 2 in. length of ¼ in. diameter dowel and glue it into a hole drilled beneath the entrance hole.

● After filling any defects and recessed pin and screw heads with epoxy filler, sand all surfaces smooth. Paint the outer walls, roof, and base with a water-based stain or varnish.

SEAT PERCH

14 Draw out the two seat ends, but, before scoring and cutting the ⅛ in. thick plywood, cut the holes for the seat slats by first drilling a row of ³⁄₃₂ in. holes and then cutting out the waste with a fretsaw. Score across the grain and carefully cut out the seat ends with the fret saw.

15 Cut three 2½ x ³⁄₃₂ in. solid slats and glue them into the slots in the seat ends. Drill the baseboard to take four fine pins and glue and pin the seat to the base. To allow the glue to stick to the wood, scrape away an area of paint from the point where the seat legs touch the base. Finish the seat with either paint or varnish.

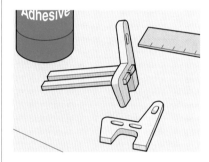

MOUNTING

16 The box can be hung on a wall by fitting a short batten to the rear of the box, or alternatively mount on a post of a similar section as the inside dimensions of the box.

MEXICAN MISSION

HUNG ON A ROUGH RENDERED WALL, AND SET OFF WITH CACTI AND SUCCULENTS,

THIS MEXICAN-STYLE MISSION HOUSE OFFERS SANCTUARY TO SMALL BIRDS SUCH

AS FINCHES AND WOODPECKERS, TO REAR THEIR YOUNG. WITH ITS REMOVABLE FLOOR AND

ENTRANCE HOLE, THE BOX CAN BE MADE TO SUIT MOST CAVITY-NESTING BIRDS, WHETHER

THEY PREFER A HOLE ENTRANCE OR OPEN-FRONTED BOXES.

MATERIALS

1 piece of 24 x 24 x ⅜ in.
plywood

1 piece of 48 x 1 in. half-
round bead

Exterior wood glue

Screws

Stain and paint

¾ in. molding pins

WALLS

1 Draw the front and back panels out on ⅜ in. plywood, following the drawing. Score across the grain and cut on the waste side of the line. Clamp both pieces in a vise, and finish the edges straight and square with a plane or file. Cut out the arched door, windows and belfry and finish the cut edges with abrasive paper wrapped over straight or rounded sanding block.

2 Cut the two side walls (4 x 7⅛ in.) and two roof sections (4 x 5¾ in.) from ⅜ in. plywood. Plane the edges square and plane a 45-deg. bevel on one end of each.

Cut the small roof section (4 x 2⅜ in.) and plane the edges square.

3 Glue and pin the side walls and roof section between the front and back walls, checking that all remains square.

4 Cut six 5 in. lengths of ¾ in. half-round bead and plane a narrow flat along each edge. Glue and pin the bead to the pitched roof.

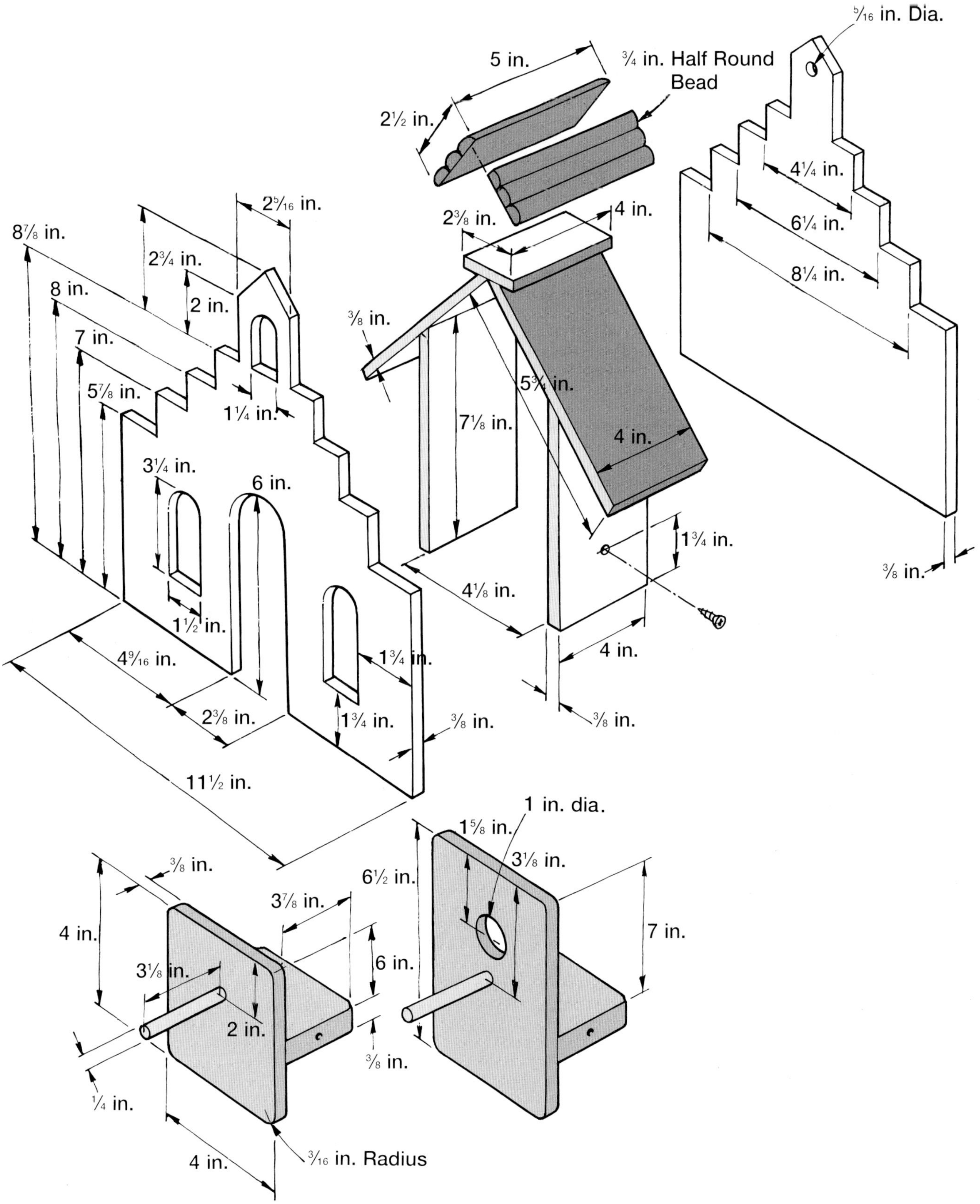
5⁄16 in. Dia.
5 in.
3⁄4 in. Half Round Bead
2 1⁄2 in.
4 1⁄4 in.
6 1⁄4 in.
8 1⁄4 in.
2 3⁄8 in.
4 in.
2 5⁄16 in.
8 7⁄8 in.
2 3⁄4 in.
8 in.
2 in.
3⁄8 in.
7 in.
5 7⁄8 in.
1 1⁄4 in.
5 3⁄4 in.
7 1⁄8 in.
4 in.
3 1⁄4 in.
6 in.
1 3⁄4 in.
3⁄8 in.
4 1⁄8 in.
1 1⁄2 in.
4 in.
4 9⁄16 in.
1 3⁄4 in.
2 3⁄8 in.
1 3⁄4 in.
3⁄8 in.
3⁄8 in.
11 1⁄2 in.
1 in. dia.
1 5⁄8 in.
3⁄8 in.
6 1⁄2 in.
3 1⁄8 in.
3 7⁄8 in.
4 in.
7 in.
6 in.
3 1⁄8 in.
2 in.
3⁄8 in.
1⁄4 in.
4 in.
3⁄16 in. Radius

5 Cut a rectangular piece of ⅜ in. plywood equal to the distance between the side walls and ½ in. higher than the door opening. Set this in the opening and draw in the opening's outline. Find the center of the arch and use it as the center point for the entrance hole. Drill the hole using a 1 in. hole saw.

6 Cut a rectangular piece of ⅜ in. plywood 4 x 3⅞ in., and trim the corners at 45 deg. (for drainage). Screw and glue this to the door panel 3 in. below the entrance hole. Depending on the bird species you wish to attract, a ¼ in. diameter perch can be added. Alternatively, the door panel can be cut lower to produce an open-fronted box. Drill through the side wall to locate the nesting floor with a brass screw or loose pin.

FINISHING TOUCHES

After filling any defects and recessed pin and screw heads with epoxy filler, sand all surfaces smooth. Paint the outer walls and roof with exterior masonry paint.

LOG CABIN

REMINISCENT OF THE CABINS USED BY BACKWOODSMEN, THIS BIRDHOUSE IS MADE OF HALF-ROUND DOWEL GLUED TO PLYWOOD END AND ROOF PANELS. THE INTERIOR HAS A REMOVABLE SECTION THAT ALLOWS YOU TO CHANGE THE SIZE OF THE INTERIOR NESTBOX TO ACCOMMODATE DIFFERENT SPECIES. FOR SMALLER SPECIES SUCH AS FINCHES, CHICADEES, WRENS, AND NUTHATCHES, FIT THE INTERIOR FLOOR AND PARTITION SECTION OR, FOR A DEEPER BOX, SIMPLY DIVIDE THE INTERNAL LENGTH.

MATERIALS

2 pieces of 84 x 1 in. diameter dowel

1 piece 12 x 3 x ¾ in. timber

1 piece of 14 x 30 x ½ in. plywood

1 piece 9 x 3 x ¾ in. timber (blocks)

1 piece of 10¼ x 3 x 1 in. timber

1 piece of 8 x ⅜ in. quarter-round bead

1 piece of 18 x 14 x ½ in. plywood

1 piece of 13½ x ¼ in. diameter dowel

1 piece of 2 x ½ in. diameter dowel

Exterior wood glue

Stain and paint

¾ in. molding pins

Screws

WALLS

1 The walls and roof of our log cabin are made from 1 in. half-round bead. Alternatively, use 1 in. dowel (or broom handle) sawn along its length.

2 Cut the two end panels from ⅜ in. plywood, scoring across the grain with a craft knife and finishing the edges square with a plane.

3 Drill the entrance hole with a hole saw to suit specific bird species.

4 Cut the half-round dowel into seven lengths and plane a narrow flat along each edge. This is to allow adequate edge width to form a horizontal glue joint between each piece. Cut one piece in half lengthways for the top rails.

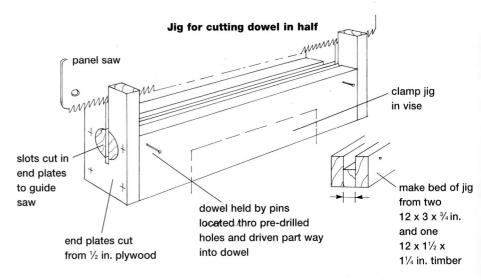

Jig for cutting dowel in half

panel saw

slots cut in end plates to guide saw

end plates cut from ½ in. plywood

dowel held by pins located thro pre-drilled holes and driven part way into dowel

clamp jig in vise

make bed of jig from two 12 x 3 x ¾ in. and one 12 x 1½ x 1¼ in. timber

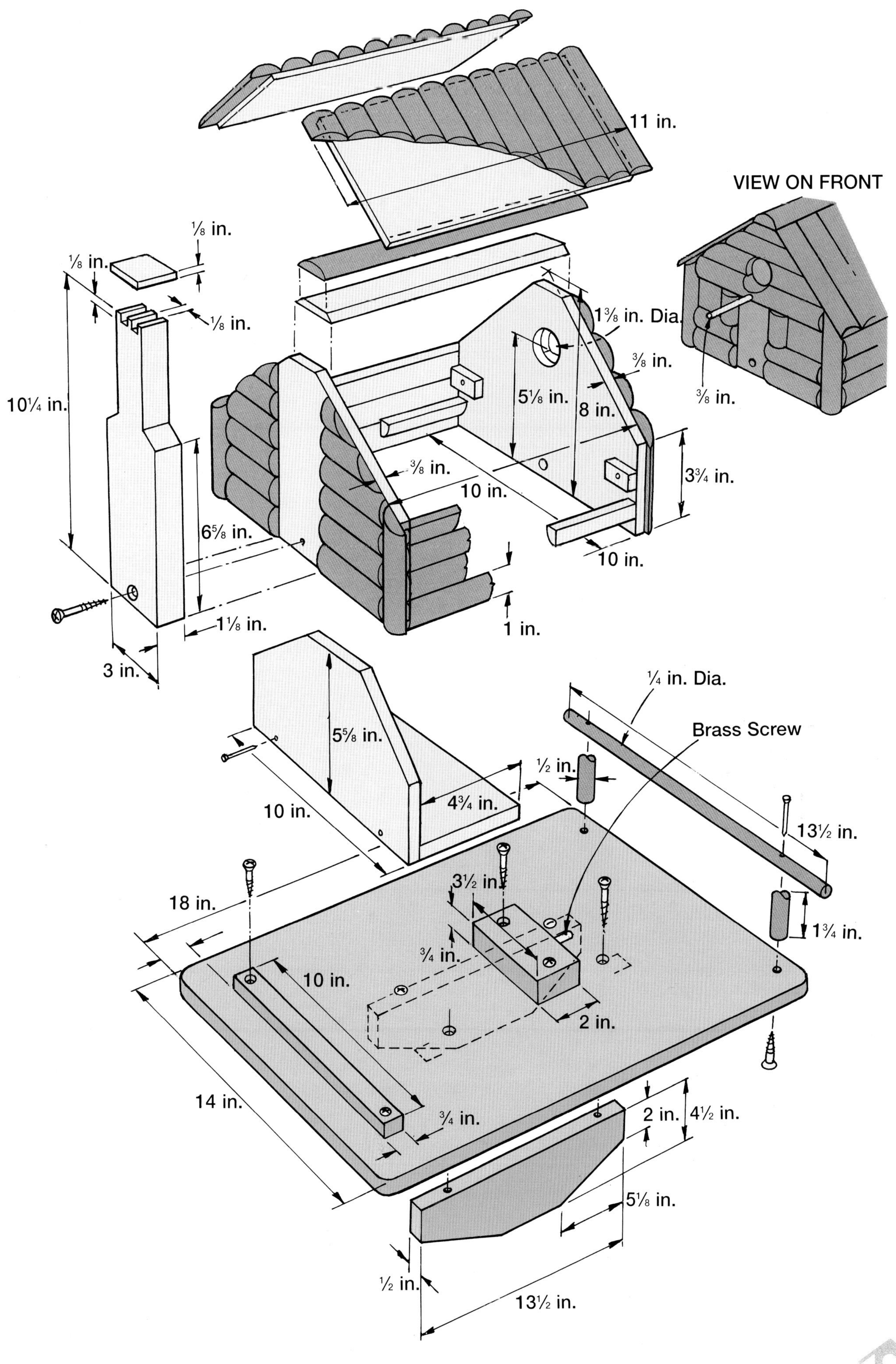
11 in.
VIEW ON FRONT
⅛ in.
⅛ in.
⅛ in.
10¼ in.
1⅜ in. Dia.
⅜ in.
5⅛ in.
8 in.
⅜ in.
⅜ in.
10 in.
3¾ in.
6⅝ in.
10 in.
1⅛ in.
1 in.
3 in.
¼ in. Dia.
Brass Screw
5⅝ in.
½ in.
10 in.
4¾ in.
13½ in.
3½ in.
18 in.
¾ in.
1¾ in.
10 in.
2 in.
14 in.
¾ in.
2 in.
4½ in.
5⅛ in.
½ in.
13½ in.

5 Glue and pin the rails to the two end pieces, gluing each horizontal joint as you proceed, and check that the end panels are vertical and square to the sides. Fit the narrow pieces at the top of the wall, and when dry plane the top edges to follow the roof angle.

● Cut tho flat oontor roof ridgo member to length from ⅛ in. plywood to finish flush with the outer face of the two end walls. Glue and pin this in place. When dry, plane the edges to match the roof angle.

7 Cut the two roof panels to size from ⅛ in. plywood , again finishing flush with the outer face of the end and side walls. Glue and pin both panels in place.

8 Cut 22 lengths of half-round dowel ¼ in. longer than the width of the angled roof panels. Glue and pin these to the roof panels, checking that no pins protrude through the underside. Arrange the pieces to leave equal overhang at either end and lay the top ends flush with the top edge of the panels.

9 Carefully cut the top corner of each piece to form a flat surface either side of the ridge board. Glue and pin a length of half-dowel flat onto the ridge board starting from the chimney end.

10 Cut the chimney from a 10¼ in. piece of 3 x 1⅛ in. wood, using a backsaw to cut partway down the length and across at an angle of 45 deg. to form the narrow section. Cut two ⅛ in. grooves at the top. Cut an ⅛ in. plywood plate slightly larger than the chimney top and glue and pin it over the grooves. Glue and screw the chimney to the end wall.

11 Cut four short lengths of half-dowel to form the vertical corner pieces and further lengths to fit between these to cover the rear wall. Repeat this on the front wall, leaving the window and door openings.

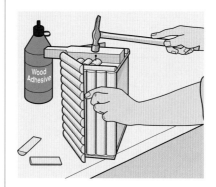

NESTING COMPARTMENT

12 Many smaller birds prefer a smaller nesting space. To encourage specific species, the inside of this box and the hole size can be adapted to suit. For larger species the nesting compartment can be omitted and the hole enlarged.

13 Cut the vertical division to fit to the underside of the roof. Cut the floor to the width of the house and glue and pin the two pieces together. Cut two 5 in. long x ⅜ in. quarter round bead, support battens slightly shorter than half the internal house length and glue them to the inside walls. The two small blocks prevent the nesting compartment from tipping back.

BASEBOARD

14 Cut the baseboard to size 14 x 18 in. from ½ in. plywood and round the four corners. Mark out and cut the two support brackets from ¾ in. wood. Screw the two pieces together and position them on the underside of the baseboard. Drill through the baseboard and glue and screw the battens to the underside.

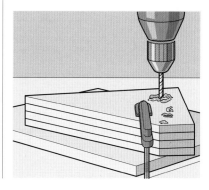

15 Cut the ¾ x ¾ in. rear locating batten to fit the full internal width of the house. Screw this batten centrally, 1½ in. from the rear edge. Cut the front-locating block and drive a

1½ in. brass screw into the center of the front face, leaving ¾ in. of the shank protruding. Cut the head off the screw with a junior hacksaw and file the edge smooth. To mark the hole position for the locating stud, rub a pencil point against the end of the screw to leave graphite deposits. Center the outside face of the door on the stud and push the house against the stud end. Use a drill of equal diameter to the stud to drill the locating hole, after transferring the mark to the outside face.

HITCHING RAIL PERCH

16 Cut the rail to length from ¼ in. diameter dowel. Cut two short lengths of ½ in. dowel (or square bead) and file a recess in one end of each to take the rail. Drill a pilot hole in the end of each post and drill and screw through the baseboard to secure them. To prevent the pins splitting the posts, drill fine pilot holes in the tops of the posts before gluing and pinning the rail to them.

Locate the stud in the hole at the front and slide the house backward to drop over the rear batten.

Secure the house with a round-headed brass screw inserted through the rear wall into the locating batten.

FINISHING TOUCHES

After filling any defects and recessed pin and screw heads with epoxy filler, sand all surfaces smooth and finish with water-based exterior stain or varnish. Paint the chimney with exterior masonry paint.

WATERWHEEL

A COMBINED BIRDBATH AND NESTING BOX, THIS DELIGHTFUL MINIATURE MILLHOUSE AND WATER WHEEL WILL ATTRACT A WIDE VARIETY OF BIRDS ALL THE YEAR ROUND. THE NESTING BOX IS SUITABLE FOR MOST SMALLER SPECIES SUCH AS CHICKADEES, FINCHES, AND WRENS. BUT DO REMEMBER TO EMPTY THE BIRDBATH, TO DISCOURAGE OTHER BIRDS FROM LANDING WHILE YOUNG ARE ON THE NEST.

MILL HOUSE

1 Draw the front entrance (3½ x 2⅛ in.) on ⅜ in. plywood, with a 45-deg. roof pitch and 2⅜ x 1½ in. opening. Score across the grain and drill a ⅜ in. diameter hole in the center waste. Use a jigsaw to cut the opening, inserting the blade through the hole. Finish the edges square with a file or abrasive paper wrapped around a square batten. Cut around the outline and plane the edges square.

2 Draw the two pairs of side walls (2⅝ x 1½ in. and 5⅝ x 3½ in.) on ⅜ in. plywood. Score across the grain on each piece and cut each to size. Clamp each pair in the vise and plane the edges square.

3 Draw the front and rear walls (6⅛ x 6 in.) on ⅜ in. plywood, with a 45-deg. roof pitch. Score across the grain on each piece and cut each to size. Clamp them together in the vise and plane to the same size, leaving the edges square. Cut out the opening in one piece to take the entrance. Do this with a jigsaw, finishing the internal edges square with a file or abrasive paper wrapped around a square batten.

4 Mark out the rebate on the edges of the front and back walls and the smaller side walls. The width of this rebate is equal to the thickness of the plywood (⅜ in.) with a depth of two veneers or a third of the thickness of the edges.

5 Score across the grain on both pieces, before cutting on the inside of the line with a backsaw, to the rebate depth. Pare the plywood veneers away with a chisel to form the rebates.

(See page 121 for tips on making a simple beam compass.)

MATERIALS

1 piece of 24 x 12 x ⅜ in. plywood
1 piece of 18 x 15 x ½ in. plywood
1 piece of 48 x 3 x ¾ in. timber
Exterior wood glue
Stain and paint
¾ in. molding pins
Screws
Terracotta dish

OTHER TOOLS

Router and ¼ in. diameter straight bit
Beam compass

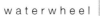

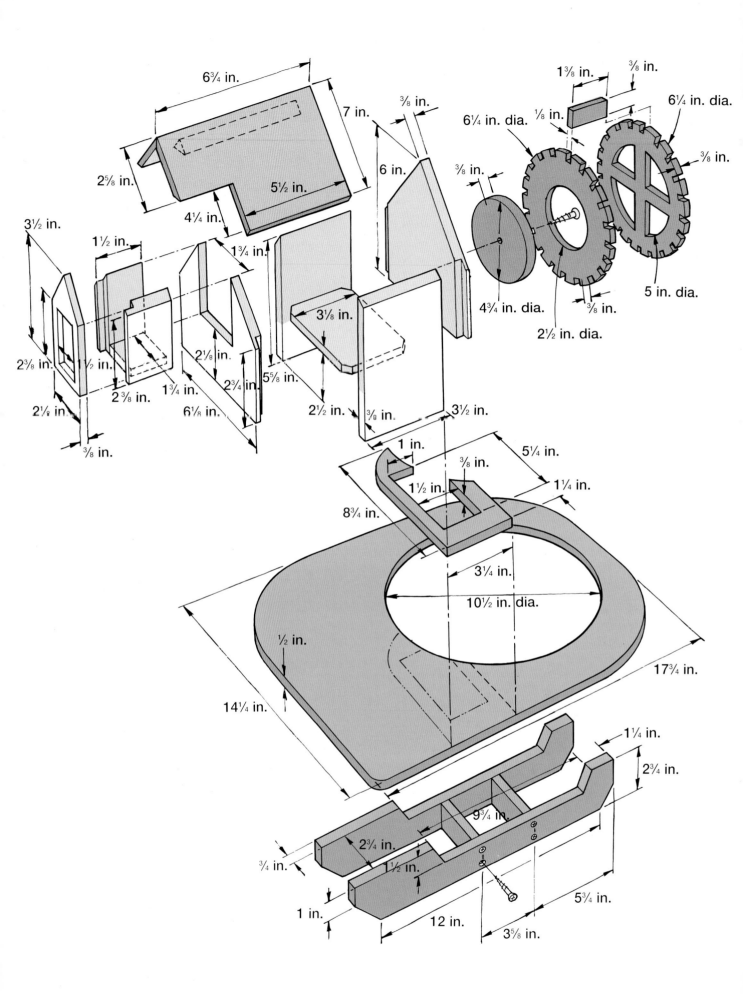

6 Glue and pin the sides together and check that the corners are square. When dry, plane or sand the edges flush and sink the pins with a punch.

7 Plane the top edges of the sides to follow the roof pitch. Cut two floors to size and angle the corners of the larger one. Glue and pin these into the mill.

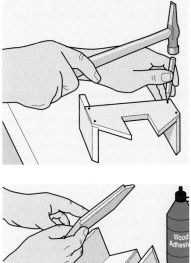

8 Mark out and cut the two L-shaped roof panels to size (6¾ x 7 in) from ⅜ in. plywood. Clamp them in the vise together and plane them to the same size, leaving the edges square.

9 Draw a line across the inside face of the two pieces, ¼ in. from the top edges and parallel. Plane to the line to leave a 45-deg. miter. Glue these edges together to form the pitched roof. Cut a square batten to the internal length of the loft and position and glue it into the apex of the roof.

W H E E L

10 Using a pair of compasses, draw the two circular wheel rims (6¼ in. diameter) and backing plate (4¾ in. diameter) on ⅜ in. plywood. Cut the wheel rims using the electric router fitted with a straight cutter and trammel point, or a jigsaw. ` The edges cut with the latter will need sanding.

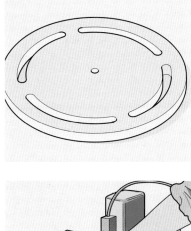

11 To hold the plywood, fasten it to a waste board by pinning through the inner and outer waste and the rim itself. This will ensure that none of the pieces will move when cut free of each other. Check that none of the pins can be caught by the router cutter or saw blade, and, when using the router, cut in a series of shallow steps before cutting to the full depth. When cutting the spokes of the front rim, score along the lines before using the jigsaw, or clamp a straight edge across the wood to guide a router.

12 Glue the backing plate to the rear rim. Mark out the spacing for 20 blades around the circumference of the front rim. Find the center of the rim with a pair of compasses and draw a circle on the face of the rim, ⅛ in. from the edge, to mark the depth of the notches. Clamp both rims together in the vise, and use a try square to extend the center lines across the edge of both rims. From these lines set out the width of each notch (³⁄₃₂ in.).

13 Drill a ³⁄₁₆ in. hole at the center of the backing plate to take a round-headed brass mounting screw.

● Use a fine backsaw to cut down either side of each notch. With a fretsaw or narrow chisel, cut out the waste from each notch.

15 Cut 20 1¼ in. lengths of ¼ x ³⁄₃₂ in. strip (it may be necessary to plane thicker material to this size). Align the notches on both rims and clamp a ¾ in. batten between them. Glue as many of the blades to the rim before it is necessary to remove the batten. At this point allow the glue on the other slat to dry before releasing the clamps. Wipe any excess glue from both the inside and outside of the wheel.

BASEBOARD

16 Set out the size of the baseboard on ½ in. plywood, using a 6 in. diameter plate or paint can to draw the three large-radius corners. Use a large coin for the fourth corner.

17 A shallow terracotta or plastic dish can be used for the birdbath, but do check that it has a ridged edge to allow it to sit level and securely in the circular cutout. Measure the diameter of the dish below the ridge level. Set out this diameter with a pair of compasses on the baseboard and check that there is room for the house and wheel.

18 Cut out the circle using either a jigsaw, or a router fitted with a trammel bar. The latter will leave the best finish and save a lot of cleaning up. Check that the dish fits before finally finishing the edge by sanding with a abrasive paper over a curved backing block. Cut around the baseboard with the jigsaw, having first scored along the curved lines, and plane or sand the edge.

19 Mark out and cut the moat surround from ½ in. plywood; sand all edges. Before painting the baseboard, temporarily screw the wheel to the mill and position the mill on the board. Position the moat under the wheel and glue it in position.

20 After filling any defects and recessed pin and screw heads with epoxy filler, sand all surfaces smooth. Paint the roof and walls with exterior masonry paint. The water wheel and baseboard can be finished with a suitable non-toxic exterior-grade varnish or stain.

21 Cut the post brackets from a piece of 2¾ x ¾ in. wood, cutting away the top edge to clear the dish. Screw the brackets and spacers together and screw the assembled bracket to the underside of the board.

22 Finally, screw the water wheel to the mill and screw the mill in place on the baseboard.

MAILBOXES

THESE TWO ATTRACTIVE NESTING-BOX DESIGNS ARE EASY TO MAKE BY BENDING THIN PLYWOOD OVER THE CURVED END PANELS. AS IT IS EASY TO ALTER THE OVERALL SIZE, THESE BOXES CAN BE MADE TO SUIT ANY BIRD SPECIES. ENTRANCE HOLES CAN ALSO BE CUT TO ANY DIAMETER, WHILE OPEN-FRONTED BOXES CAN BE FORMED BY CUTTING A SEMICIRCULAR HOLE.

SITE THEM ON WALLS OR FENCE POSTS WITH A SMALL SUPPLY OF NESTING MATERIAL IN THEM. LEAVE OTHER NESTING MATERIAL SUCH AS MOSS, HAIR, AND SHORT LENGTHS OF WOOL AND COTTON CLOSE BY. TO CLEAN OUT, SIMPLY LIFT THE BOX FROM ITS BRACKETS AND BRUSH OFF THE OLD NESTING MATERIAL. WASH THE INSIDE OF THE BOX WITH HOT SOAPY WATER TO RID IT OF MITES.

MATERIALS

SMALL
1 piece of 18 x 3 x ¾ in. timber
1 piece 2 x ½ in. half-round bead
1 piece 18 x 18 x ⅜ in. plywood
1 piece 21¼ x 6 x ⅛ in. plywood

LARGE
1 piece of 7 x 3 x ¾ in. timber
1 x 3 x ¼ in. diameter dowel
1 piece 24 x 24 x ⅜ in. plywood
1 piece of 30 x 8 x ⅛ in. plywood
Exterior wood glue
Screws
Stain or paint
¾ in. molding pins

FRONT AND BACK

1 Draw the front and back panels on to ⅜ in. plywood, setting out the curved top with a pair of compasses.

2 Score across the grain on both pieces and cut out with a jigsaw. Clamp the two pieces in the vise together. Finish the straight edges with a plane and the curved section with a rasp, or a sanding block and abrasive paper.

3 Cut the entrance hole with a hole saw of 1 to 1¼ in. to suit specific bird species. If required, cut a 2 in. length of ¼ in. diameter dowel and glue it into a hole drilled beneath the entrance hole. On the rear panel cut the V-shaped cutout.

4 Alternatively, a small platform can be screwed to the front of the box with a short bead fitted to its edge. To shelter the entrance hole, cut a small piece of plywood and bevel the rear edge. Fasten it above the entrance hole by screwing through from the back of the front panel.

5 Cut a piece of ⅛ in. plywood with the face grain running across the narrow width.

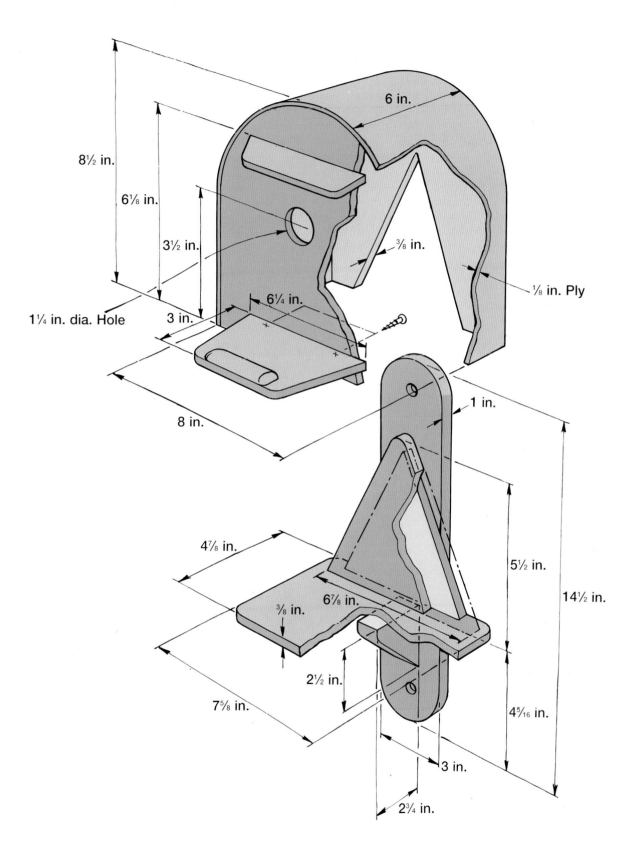

8½ in.

6⅛ in.

3½ in.

1¼ in. dia. Hole

3 in.

6¼ in.

6 in.

⅜ in.

⅛ in. Ply

8 in.

1 in.

4⅞ in.

⅜ in.

6⅞ in.

5½ in.

14½ in.

2½ in.

7⅝ in.

4⁵⁄₁₆ in.

3 in.

2¾ in.

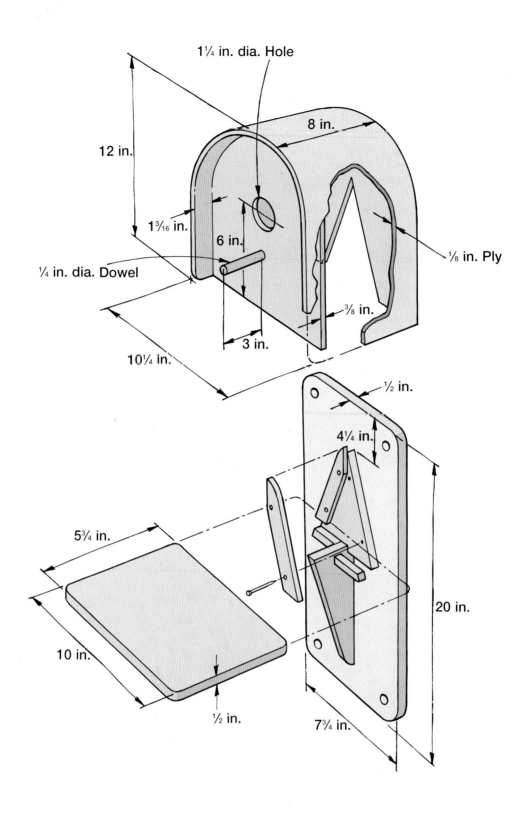

1¼ in. dia. Hole

8 in.

12 in.

1³⁄₁₆ in.

6 in.

¼ in. dia. Dowel

⅛ in. Ply

³⁄₈ in.

3 in.

10¼ in.

½ in.

4¼ in.

5¾ in.

10 in.

20 in.

½ in.

7¾ in.

6 Mark the very center of the top of the arch on the front and rear panels and draw a center line across the width of the roof panel.

7 Run a ribbon of glue around the edges of the rear panel. Drive a pin through the top panel on the center line (either on the edge or set 1 in. back from the edge if a overhang is required). Align the center line on the roof panel with the center line on the rear panel and gently bend the plywood around the curved top edge. Use C-clamps, a webbing clamp, or cord tourniquet to gradually pull it down evenly, while securing it with pins.

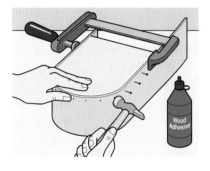

8 Cut three blocks of wood equal in length to the final internal width of the box and stand them against the internal sides. Run a ribbon of glue around the edges of the front panel and rest it on top of the three blocks. Secure the front panel into the box as before.

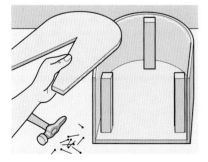

9 When dry, plane the bottom edges flush and, if the front edge overhangs, round the bottom front corners of the curved panel.

10 The top of the box is designed to lift off its mounting bracket, leaving the nest base. Cut the mounting bracket from either a piece of 3 x 1 in. wood or as a ⅜ in. plywood plate. Cut the plate to size and cut the ends or corners round.

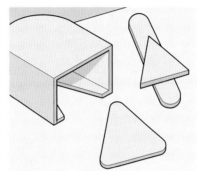

11 Cut two triangular plates, one to fit into the V-shaped cutout in the back of the box, the other wider by a ¼ in. on each edge. Alternatively, battens can be screwed to the edges of the smaller plate. The base of the nesting box is cut to fit its internal dimensions from ⅜ in. plywood. Cut out the base and round the corners. Glue and pin the base to the top triangular plate or to two short battens glued and pinned to the smaller one.

FINISHING TOUCHES

After filling any defects and recessed pin and screw heads with epoxy filler, sand all surfaces smooth. Paint the outer walls, roof, and base with a water-based stain, varnish, or masonry paint.

COVERED WAGON

A REMINDER OF AMERICA'S PAST, THE COVERED WAGON IS AS MUCH HOME

TO A FAMILY OF HOUSE WRENS, ROBINS, OR TREE SWALLOWS AS IT WAS

TO THE ORIGINAL PIONEERS AND SETTLERS. DOUBLE-ENDED, IT MAY EVEN ATTRACT PURPLE

MARTINS OR OTHER COLONY NESTING BIRDS.

1 From ¼ in. plywood, cut two 8 x 8½ in. and one 8 x 9⅛ in. panels. On each panel, draw crossed center lines. On one panel only, use a pair of compasses to swing an 8 in. diameter circle from the center point. Along one edge measure 3⅜ in. either side of the center line. Draw a line from the two points, meeting the circle at a tangent on either edge.

3 Lay the cut panel over the others in turn and draw around it. Cut the other panels to the same curve.

4 At the center of the two smaller panels cut a 1¼ in. diameter entrance hole.

5 On the center panel cut a 1⅛ x ¾ in. notch at each corner.

MATERIALS

1 piece of 48 x 24 x ⅜ in. plywood

1 piece of 21¾ x 18 x ⅛ in. plywood

1 piece of 12 x ⅜ x ⅛ in. timber bead

1 piece of 18 x 2¼ x ¾ in. timber

1 piece of 60 x ¼ x ¼ in. timber bead

1 piece of 60 x ⅜ x ⅜ in. timber bead

Exterior wood glue

Screws

Stain and paint

¾ in. molding pins

OTHER TOOLS

Webbing clamps

Beam compass

Lathe

Router

(see page 121 for how to make a beam compass)

End and centre division details

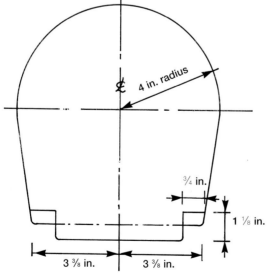

mark center line on face

4 in. radius

¾ in.

1 ⅛ in.

3 ⅜ in. 3 ⅜ in.

2 Use a craft knife to score the full length of the line before cutting along the waste side with a jigsaw.

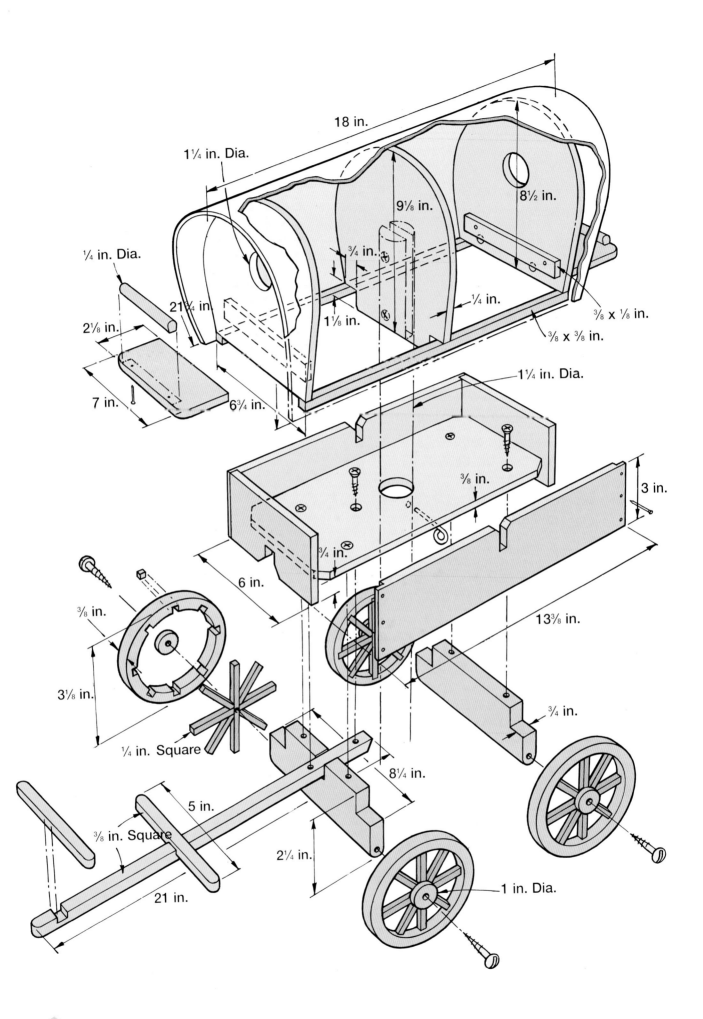

18 in.

1¼ in. Dia.

¼ in. Dia.

9⅛ in.

8½ in.

2⅛ in.

21¾ in

¾ in.

1⅛ in.

¼ in.

⅜ x ⅛ in.

⅜ x ⅜ in.

7 in.

6¾ in.

1¼ in. Dia.

3 in.

⅜ in.

¾ in.

6 in.

13⅜ in.

⅜ in.

¾ in.

3⅛ in.

¼ in. Square

8¼ in.

5 in.

⅜ in. Square

2¼ in.

21 in.

1 in. Dia.

6 From ⅛ in. plywood cut a 21¾ x 18 in. rectangular panel with the grain running along the longer length. Draw a center line across the 18 in. width and center lines for each of the three curved divisions, at right angles to it.

7 Run a ribbon of glue along each center line. Align the top center of the middle curved division against the center line on the panel and pin the panel to it. Carefully wrap the plywood part way around the curve and secure with clamps or a cord tourniquet. Fit and pin the two end divisions in a similar manner. Working on one side at a time, tighten the plywood against the divisions, pinning it at 1 in. intervals. Regularly tighten the clamps as you fasten further around the curve. Clean off any excess glue and leave the clamps in place until the glue has dried thoroughly.

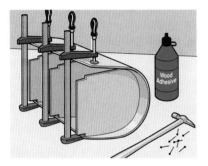

8 To mark the splayed end of the canopy, wrap a strip of plastic or card around the curve at one end, positioning it against the edge at the top center. Pull the ends back to meet the bottom edge at a point ¼ in. in front of the division. Draw a

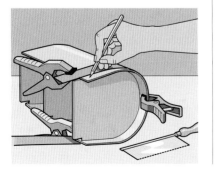

line along the edge of the strip and repeat the procedure at the other end. Score along the line and cut the splay with a fine-toothed backsaw.

9 After scoring with a craft knife, use a coping saw to trim the bottom edges of the two end divisions level, ⅜ in. above the bottom edges of the curved top.

10 Cut two ⅜ x ⅜ in. strips and glue them along the bottom edge of the canopy.

11 On the inside ends of the canopy, glue two full-width battens ⅜ x ⅛ in., positioned to rest on the wagon ends when the canopy is fitted.

12 Cut two 7 x 2⅛ in. footboards from ⅜ in. plywood and glue and pin them to the end panels of the canopy. Glue and pin a length of ¼ in. diameter dowel to the front edge of each board.

WAGON

13 Cut four strips of 3 x ⅜ in. plywood, two 13⅜ in. long and two 6 in. long. Mark out and cut ⅜ x 3⁄16 in. rebates at the ends of the short lengths. Glue and pin the four pieces together, checking that the corners are square.

14 Cut the wagon floor from ⅜ in. plywood and trim all four corners at 45 deg. (for drainage). Glue the floor into the frame, raising it ¾ in. up from the bottom edge.

15 Cut two 8¼ x 2¼ x ¾ in. battens. Hold the battens in turn in a vise and round over one edge with a plane. Cut a notch at the end of each batten to allow them to be glued to the underside of the floor. On one batten, cut a notch, centered along the square edge, to allow the "trace" to pass through. Glue the battens in place.

16 Using the canopy as a guide, mark the position of the notches on both sides of the wagon to receive the center division when the canopy is filled. Cut the notches and chamfer the top corners.

TRACES

17 Cut one 21 x ⅜ x ⅜ in. and two 5 x ⅜ x ⅜ in. battens. Along the longer piece, set out and cut two ⅜ x 3⁄16 in. notches to take the short lengths. Round over the ends of the short lengths, and glue and screw them in place. On the front of the wagon, cut a notch to allow the trace to be glued and screwed to the underside of the floor.

WHEELS

18 Mark out on ⅜ in. plywood each of the four wheel rims and divide them into 12 equal segments. Mark out the width of each of the notches to take the spokes.

19 Cut out the wheel rims using the electric router fitted with a trammel point, set to a radius of 3⅛ in. Reset the radius to leave a rim width of ⅝ in. and cut the inner diameter. Remember to secure both the inner and outer waste as well as the rim, before cutting.

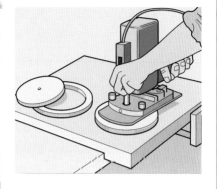

20 With the rims clamped in the vise together, cut across the notches on all four at the same time, taking the waste out with a number of saw cuts. Square up the notches with a narrow file or chisel.

21 Cut the spokes to length from ¼ in. square strip. The first spoke is glued into notches on opposite sides of the rim. The remaining spokes are cut and/or mitered to be glued at the center. The remaining part of the notch can be filled with epoxy filler and sanded.

Turn four 1 in. hub disks on a lathe or cut them from thin material with a fret saw. Glue each disk to the center of the spokes. Drill a hole through each hub to take a round-headed brass screw.

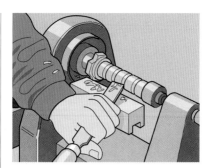

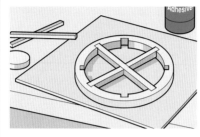

MOUNTING

22 Mount the wagon on a 3 x 3 in. post held by angle brackets or blocks screwed to the underside of the floor. Alternatively drill a 1³⁄₁₆ in. diameter hole through the underside of the wagon, to take an 18 in. length of 1¼ in. diameter dowel. Cut a 4 x ⅜ in. notch down the center of the dowel, and glue and screw it to the center division of the wagon. This allows the wagon to drop away from the canopy for cleaning out. Lift the wagon up tight beneath the canopy and mark the underside of the canopy. Remove the wagon and drill the dowel to take a ⅛ in. diameter locking pin, made from bent brass rod or similar. Drill the top of the mounting post (3 in. round or square) to allow the dowel to be inserted at least 5 in. Secure the dowel in the post with a long wood screw.

FINISHING TOUCHES

After filling any defects and recessed pin and screw heads with epoxy filler, sand all surfaces smooth. Paint the canopy with exterior masonry paint and the wagon sides with a water-based stain or varnish.

LAMP HOUSE

MOUNTED ON A THIN METAL POLE, THIS SIMPLE GEOMETRIC DESIGN IS MADE AS TWO SIMPLE PLYWOOD PYRAMIDS, FASTENED TOGETHER WITH BRASS HOOKS AND EYES.

THE LARGER TOP SECTION OVERHANGS THE BASE TO SHED RAINWATER AWAY FROM THE ENTRANCE HOLE AND ALLOW THE TOP TO BE REMOVED FOR CLEANING. WITH AN ENTRANCE HOLE OF SMALL DIAMETER. IT IS IDEAL FOR ALL SMALLER SPECIES SUCH AS CHICKADEES, FINCHES, WRENS, AND WOODPECKERS.

MATERIALS

1 piece of 30 x 24 x ⅜ in. plywood

A 1 in. diameter wooden knob

1 piece of 80 x ¼ in. diameter dowel

Brass hooks and eyes

Exterior wood glue

Stain and paint

¾ in. molding pins

TOP SECTION

1 Draw the four triangular segments of the top (base 11 ⅜ x height 9 ⅝ in.) on a piece of ⅜ in. plywood with the grain running along their length and the wide and narrow ends alternated. Leave a gap of ⅛ in. between each to allow for the width of the saw blade. Score across the grain along the angled edges before cutting.

2 Cut out each segment and mark one face of each (this will be the inside face when the segments are glued together). Stack all four together in a vise, and plane all to the same size with all the edges square.

3 Stand two of the sides together with their bases at 90 deg. to each other. Measure the gap left between the two edges on the inside face. Draw a line parallel to the right-hand edge on each marked face, equal to this dimension. Plane a bevel down to this line on each of the four edges. Tape the pyramid together and check that each pair of edges mate along their full length. Glue and pin the joints together.

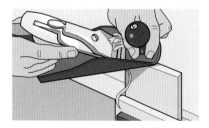

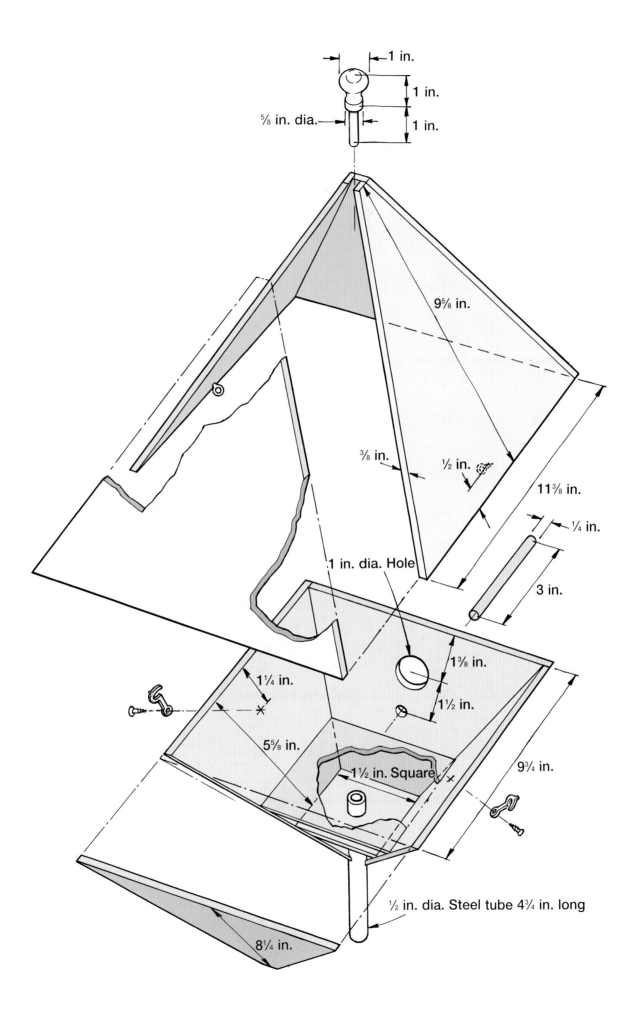

1 in.

1 in.

1 in.

⅝ in. dia.

9⅝ in.

⅜ in.

½ in.

11⅜ in.

¼ in.

3 in.

1 in. dia. Hole

1⅜ in.

1½ in.

1¼ in.

5⅝ in.

9¾ in.

1½ in. Square

½ in. dia. Steel tube 4¾ in. long

8¼ in.

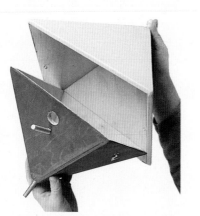

After filling any defects and recessed pin heads with epoxy filler, sand all surfaces smooth. Paint the outer walls, roof, and base with water-based stain or a non-toxic paint.

4 When dry, plane the joint edges flush and the bottom edge straight and level.

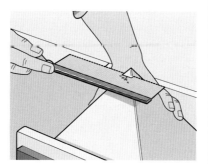

5 Cut the tip of the top pyramid to form a flat area and drill a ⅜ in. hole. Glue a turned finial or knob into the hole.

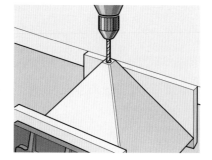

BOTTOM SECTION

6 Draw the four triangular segments of the bottom (base 9¾ in. x height 8¼ in.) and repeat the procedure as for constructing the top.

7 Cut two squares of ⅜ in. plywood 2¾ x 2¾ in. and 1½ x 1½ in. On one face of each, draw a line ¼ in. from each edge. Plane a bevel along each edge finishing on the line.

8 Mark and drill a ½ in. hole at the center of the smaller of the two squares, and glue the square into the pyramid. The second larger square is laid loose in the pyramid and forms the bottom of the box.

9 Cut a 1 in. diameter entrance hole with a drill-mounted holesaw. Cut a 3 in. length of ¼ in. diameter dowel and glue it into a hole drilled beneath the entrance hole.

10 Screw two brass hooks on opposite sides of the bottom pyramid, to locate into screw eyes fitted to the underside of the top section.

MOUNTING

11 Cut the tip of the bottom pyramid to form a flat area and drill a ½ in. hole to take a ½ in. diameter aluminum pole. Glue the pole into the base with an epoxy glue.

BEACH HUT

THE BASIC PITCHED-ROOF NESTING BOX IS GIVEN A TOUCH OF CLASS WITH

THE ADDITION OF DECORATIVE BARGEBOARDS. THIS BOX IS SUITABLE FOR

MANY LARGER BIRDS SUCH AS ROBINS, FLICKERS, AND BLUEBIRDS, BUT WILL BE JUST AS

APPEALING TO THE SMALLER VARIETIES.

MATERIALS

1 piece of 24 x 18 x ¼ in. plywood
1 piece of 12 x 1 x ⅛ in. plywood
1 piece of 6 x ½ x ½ in. triangular bead
Exterior wood glue
Stain and paint
¾ in. molding pins

WALLS

1 Cut two 5½ x 7 in. and two 9½ x 6¼ in. pieces from ¼ in. plywood.

2 Clamp the two smaller panels in the vise and plane to same size, leaving the edges square.

3 Draw on the larger two the 45-deg. roof pitch. Score across the grain and cut to this angle. Clamp together in the vise and plane to the same size, leaving edges square.

4 Mark out the rebate on the vertical inside face of the front and back. These are equal to the thickness of the plywood (¼ in.) on the inside face of each piece and a depth of ⅛ in.

5 Score across the grain on both pieces, before cutting to the depth on the inside of the line. Pare the plywood veneers away with a chisel to form the rebates.

6 Pin the four walls together, checking the bottom edges are flush and the corners are square.

7 When dry, plane the top edge of the side walls to follow the front- and rear-wall roof angle.

8 Cut the floor from ¼ in. plywood, to a push fit inside the walls. Plane the edges square and trim the corners at 45 deg. (for drainage). Drill the four walls and screw the floor in place.

9 Draw a center line down the front face. Drill the entrance hole with a 1–1¼ in. holesaw to suit a specific species.

ROOF

10 Cut the two 6 x 8 in. roof panels from ¼ in. plywood. Clamp both together in the vise and plane to the same size leaving the edges

11 On one face of each panel draw a line ¼ in. in from one long edge. Plane down to the line to produce a 45-deg. bevel along the

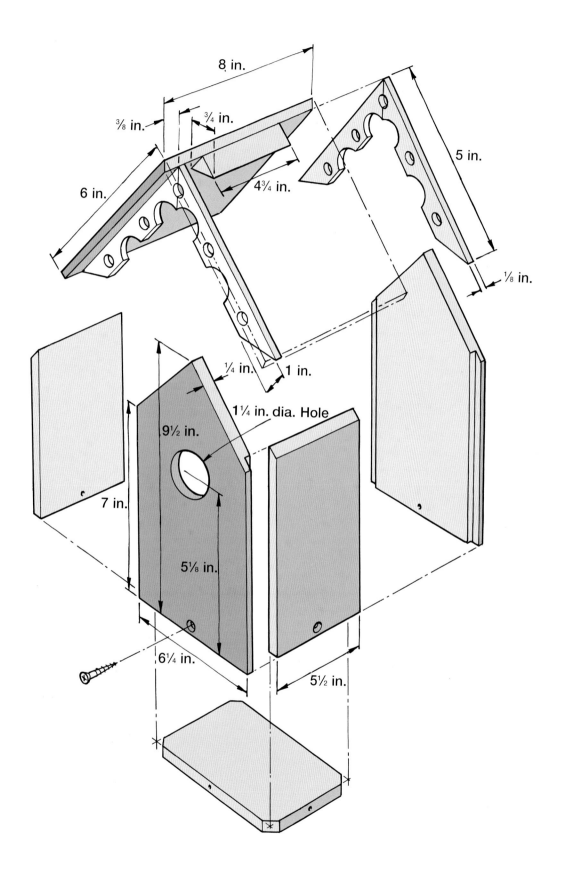

8 in.

3/8 in.

3/4 in.

6 in.

4 3/4 in.

5 in.

1/8 in.

1/4 in.   1 in.

1 1/4 in. dia. Hole

9 1/2 in.

7 in.

5 1/8 in.

6 1/4 in.

5 1/2 in.

12 Cut a 4¾ x ½ x ½ in. triangular bead and glue it against the bevelled edge of one panel, centered across the width. Glue and pin the panels together to form the pitched roof.

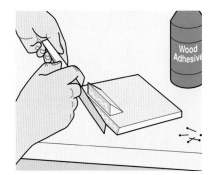

BARGEBOARDS

13 Cut four lengths of ⅛ x 1 x 5 in. plywood. Divide each length into nine equal divisions ½ in. apart and mark these with a pencil. At alternate divisions, drill a ⅛ in. diameter hole, and at the others cut a semicircular cutout using a fretsaw or router cutter.

14 Cut the miters on each end of the strips, and glue to the underside ⅛ in. back and parallel to the pitched edges of the roof.

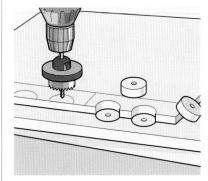

MOUNTING

16 Mount this birdhouse in among the stems of a mature wisteria or other similar wall-climbing plant. Alternatively, it can be wall-mounted in a niche or on a simple bracket.

FINISHING TOUCHES

After filling any defects and recessed pin and screw heads with epoxy filler, sand all surfaces smooth. Paint the outer walls, roof, and base with non-toxic stain or varnish and paint the bargeboards white.

COUNTRY
COTTAGE

BASED ON A TYPICAL COUNTRY COTTAGE, ITS QUAINT AND NOSTALGIC STYLE FITS WELL INTO ANY COUNTRY GARDEN. SURROUND IT WITH HERBS OR WILD FLOWERS TO ADD TO THE COUNTRY SCENE, AND TO ATTRACT MOST SMALL SPECIES OF CAVITY-NESTING BIRDS.

MATERIALS

1 piece of 30 x 18 x ⅜ in. plywood
1 piece of 12 x 12 x ¼ in. plywood
1 piece of 5 x 1½ x 1 ½ in. timber
Exterior wood glue
Stain/varnish
¾ in. molding pins

1 Draw out the two end walls, 5⅛ in. wide by 6 in. high, on ⅜ in. plywood. Set out the 45-deg. roof angle and score across the grain before cutting. Clamp both pieces together in the vise and plane to the same size, leaving all the edges square.

2 Draw out the front and rear walls, 10¼ in. wide by 4 in. high, on ⅜ in. plywood. Set out the window and door positions and score across the grain before cutting. Clamp both together in the vise and plane to the same size, leaving the edges square. Plane the top edge at an angle of 45 deg.

3 Mark out the rebate on the vertical inside face of the front and back. These are equal to the thickness of the plywood (⅜ in.) on the inside face of each piece, with a depth of ³⁄₁₆ in.

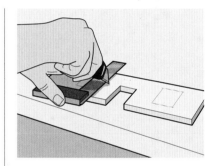

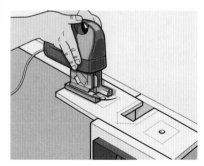

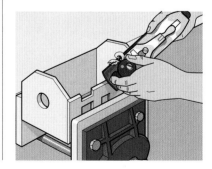

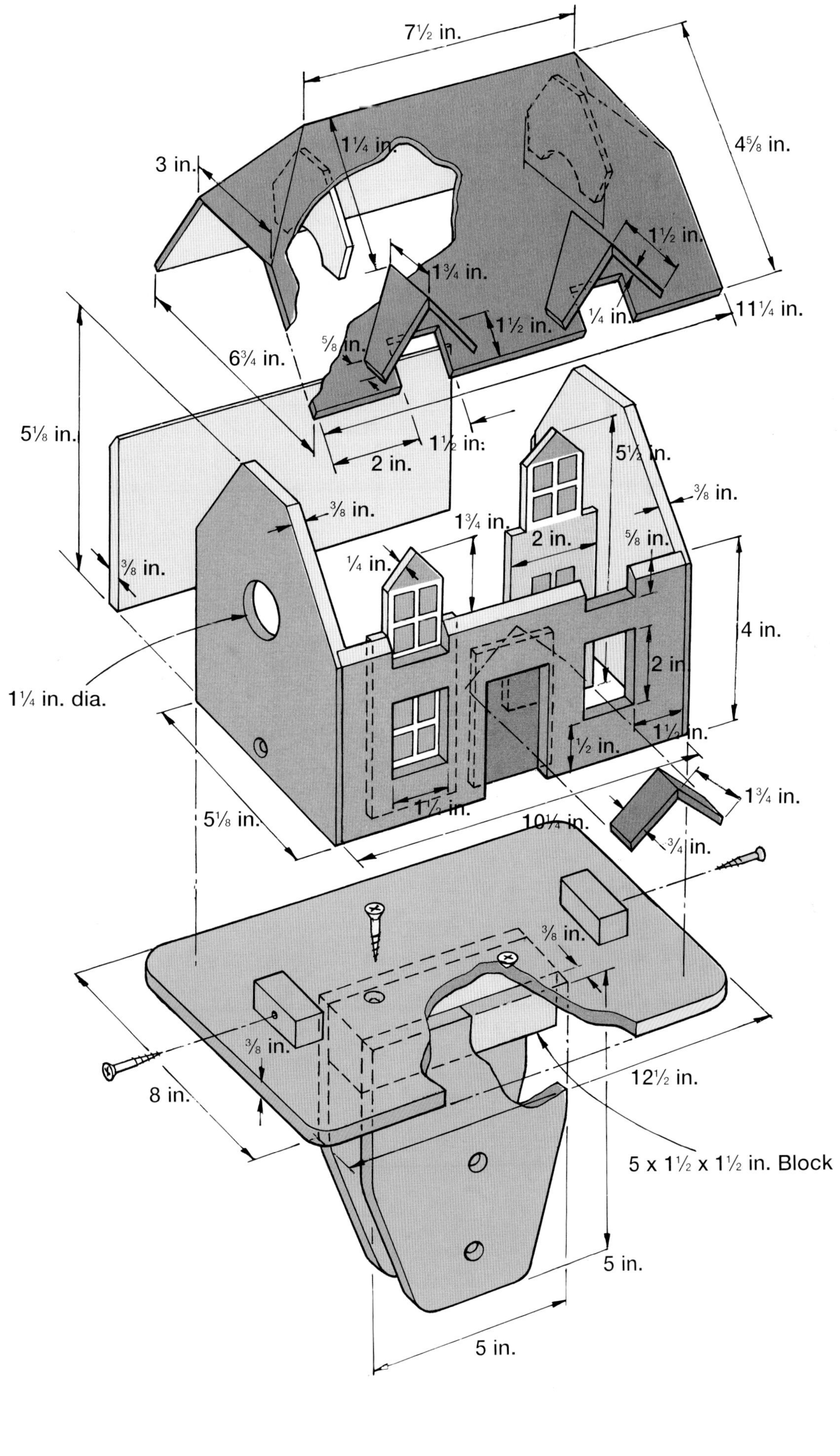

7½ in.
4⅝ in.
1¼ in.
3 in.
1½ in.
1¾ in.
1½ in.
¼ in.
11¼ in.
⅝ in.
6¾ in.
5⅛ in.
1½ in.
2 in.
5½ in.
⅜ in.
⅜ in.
1¾ in.
2 in.
⅝ in.
⅜ in.
¼ in.
4 in.
2 in.
1¼ in. dia.
1½ in.
½ in.
1¾ in.
1½ in.
5⅛ in.
10¼ in.
¾ in.
⅜ in.
⅜ in.
8 in.
12½ in.
5 x 1½ x 1½ in. Block
5 in.
5 in.

4 Draw a center line down the front face and cut the entrance hole with a 1–1¼ in. hole saw to suit specific species.

5 Score across the grain on both pieces, before cutting with a backsaw to the full depth on the inside of the line. Pare the plywood veneers away with a chisel to form the rebates.

6 Glue and pin the four walls together checking that the bottom edges are flush and that the corners are square.

ROOF

7 From ⅜ in. plywood, cut two 11¼ x 4⅝ in. roof panels and score across the grain. Cut out both sections, clamp them together in the vise and plane to the same size, leaving the edges square. Cut two 90-deg. triangular pieces of ¼ in. plywood 3 in. wide.

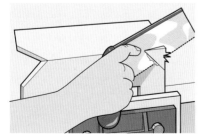

8 Along one edge on each end section, plane a 45-deg. angle. Glue and pin the two sections together. When dry, position the roof on the walls and mark out the angled ends. Hold the work in a vise and score across the grain before cutting to

the lines. Sand the cut edges flat and glue two triangular plates across the angles. When dry, sand or plane the edges flush with the roof surface.

9 Position the roof on the walls and mark the position and width of the windows along the front edge. Mark the line of the front wall on the underside of the roof. Use a try square to continue these positions up the underside of the roof slope beyond the eaves and thickness of the wall. Draw a line ¼ in. back from the inside wall, score across the grain, and cut out the dormer window openings in the roof.

10 From ¼ in. plywood, cut the two dormer window roof panels 2½ in. long x 1½ in. wide. Measure ⅝ in. along from each end but on opposite edges, and draw a line across the faces. Score and cut along the line. Along the meeting edges of the roof panels, plane a 45-deg. angle and glue them together. When dry, sand the rear edge of each roof until they sit flat against the face of the main roof.

WINDOWS AND DOOR

11 Cut two pieces of ¼ in. plywood, 2 in. wide x 7 in. long. On one end of each mark the center and cut at 45 deg. to either side. Cut the edges of the strip to allow it to slide up to the dormer roof. Check that the angle fits to the underside of the dormer roof.

12 Repeat this on the other strip and, with the roof on the walls, glue both in position. Cut a blank piece of plywood larger than the door opening and glue it to the rear face of the wall over the door opening.

13 Cut the two ¾ x 1¾ in. sides of the porch roof, from ¼ in. plywood, and plane one end of each to an angle of 45 deg. Glue these faces together and glue the porch to the wall face above the door.

BASEBOARD AND MOUNTING

14 Cut the 8 x 12½ in. baseboard from ⅜ in. plywood and radius the corners. Position the walls on the board and mark the line of the inside face of the end walls. Screw two short battens against the lines. After painting, locate the cottage over the battens and screw through predrilled and countersunk holes in the end walls.

15 Cut out the two angle mounting plates from 5 x 5 x ⅜ in. plywood. Cut a 5 x 1½ x 1½ in. long block and glue and screw the two plates either side of it. Mount the cottage on a 1½ in. square post, fitted between the plates and held by two screws from each face.

FINISHING TOUCHES

After filling any defects and recessed pin and screw heads with epoxy filler, sand all surfaces smooth. Paint the outer walls and roof with a masonry paint and finish the baseboard with a water-based stain.

MEDIEVAL TOURNAMENT TENT

CHICKADEES, WRENS, AND NUTHATCHES WILL BE JOUSTING TO WIN THE TENANCY OF THIS MEDIEVAL TOURNAMENT TENT. FIXED IN A CONVENIENT NICHE IN A STONE WALL OR MOUNTED ON A WROUGHT-IRON BRACKET, ITS SUBTLE, COLORED STRIPES WILL BLEND IN WITH THE LICHENS AND MOSSES TO ATTRACT A WIDE RANGE OF BIRDS. USE AN ENTRANCE HOLE DIAMETER OF 1⅛ TO 1½ IN. TO PREVENT LARGER BIRDS FROM MOVING IN.

MATERIALS

1 piece of 30 x 20 x ¼ in.
plywood
1 piece of 4 x 4 x 2 in.
timber
1 piece of 1½ x ¼ in.
diameter dowel
Exterior wood glue
Stain/varnish
¾ in. molding pins
1 wooden bead

SIDES

❶ Cut the six 10½ x 5½ in. sides, from ¼ in. plywood and mark one face of each (this will be the inside face when the sides are glued together). Stack all six together in a vise, and plane all to the same size, leaving all the edges square.

❷ Use a sliding bevel to accurately mark a 60-deg. angle on one edge of two of the sides and draw a line between the points across the face.

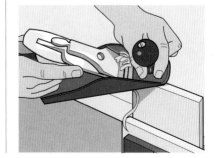

Bevel the edges of these two sides by planing down to the line, taking care not to decrease their width. Use this angle as a guide and adjust it by planing a fine shaving from the edge, until each pair of edges mate along the full length of the joint, with their bases set at an angle of 120 deg.

❸ Measure the distance of the planed line from the edge and mark the other pieces in a similar fashion. Check that each joint mates along its full length.

❹ Draw a center line down the front face of one side. Cut the entrance hole with a hole saw, depending on the size of the bird species you wish to attract (see page 143 for entrance dimensions).

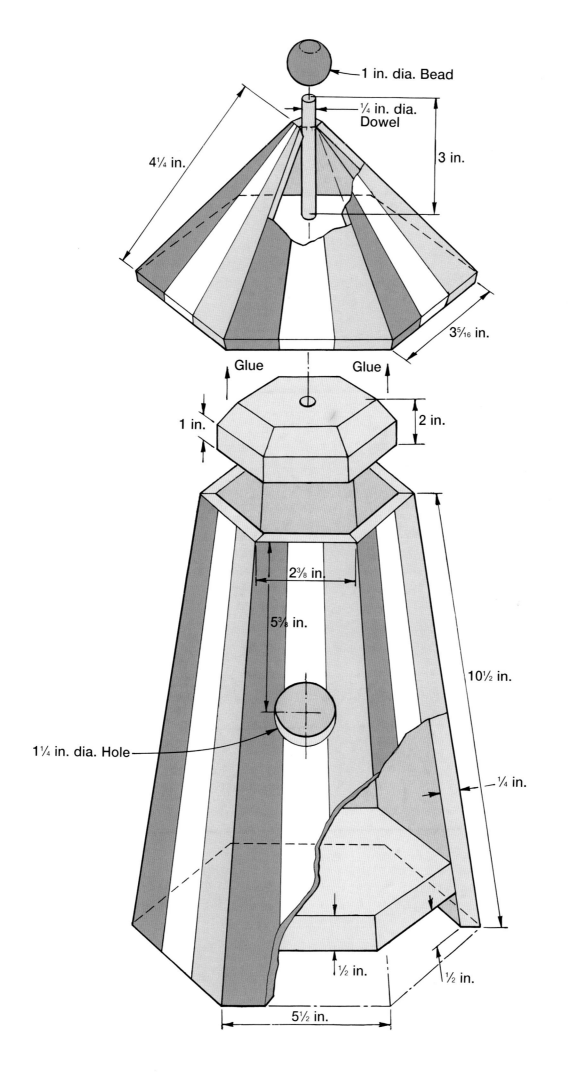

1 in. dia. Bead

¼ in. dia. Dowel

4¼ in.

3 in.

3⁵⁄₁₆ in.

Glue

Glue

1 in.

2 in.

2³⁄₈ in.

5³⁄₈ in.

10½ in.

1¼ in. dia. Hole

¼ in.

½ in.

½ in.

5½ in.

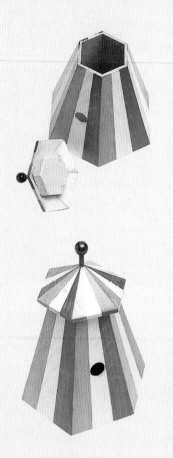

FINISHING TOUCHES

After filling any defects and recessed pin holes with epoxy filler, sand all surfaces smooth. Paint the outer walls with differently colored water-based stains, masking the edges of each strip in turn with masking tape. Finally apply a coat of a clear, water-based, exterior-grade varnish over the external surfaces.

MOUNTING

Mount this birdhouse in among the stems of a mature wisteria or other similar wall-climbing plant. Alternatively it can be wall-mounted in a niche or bracket, or on a post. To fix it securely, screw a small wooden block or metal (brass or aluminum) angle to the underside.

5 Glue and tape the six sides together, checking that each opposite pair of sides is parallel and the diagonal dimensions are equal.

6 Draw a hexagon, on a piece of ½ in. plywood, with each side measuring ⅛ in. less than the internal hexagonal base of the tent. With a sliding bevel, measure the vertical angle of the tent sides and plane the edges of the base to this angle. Check that the base fits into the tent leaving a lip of around ½ in. Glue the base into the tent.

7 When dry, stand the tent on a flat surface and draw a level line around the base. Hold the tent in a vise and plane down to the line, leaving a lip of at least ³⁄₁₆ in. Plane the top edge level in a similar way.

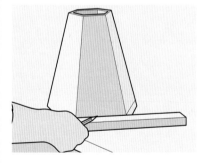

8 Cut six triangular sides, from ⅛ in. plywood and mark one face of each (this will be the inside face when the segments are glued together). Stack all six together in a vise, and plane all to the same size leaving all the edges square.

9 Using a sliding bevel to accurately mark a 60-deg. angle on one edge of two of the sides and draw a line between the points across the face. Bevel the edge of these two sides by planing down to the line, taking care not to decrease their width to any great extent. Use this angle as a guide and adjust it by planing a fine shaving from the edge, until each pair of edges mate along the full length of the joint, with their bases set at an angle of 120 deg. Glue and tape the pieces together, checking that they meet correctly at the top.

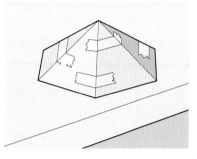

10 Measure the internal size of the hexagonal opening in the top of the tent. Draw out a hexagon to this size, on a piece of 2 in. thick wood. Plane the edges around one face to the internal angle of the roof. Glue the hexagonal block into the roof.

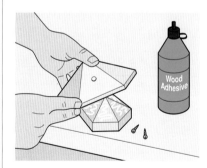

11 Drill a ¼ in. diameter hole through the apex of the roof into the block. Glue a 3 x ¼ in. length of dowel into the hole and glue a plastic or wooden bead to the top.

medieval tournament tent

WITCH'S HOUSE

A SPELLBINDING DESIGN THAT WILL ADD A MAGICAL AND MYSTICAL THEME TO YOUR GARDEN AND ENTICE A WIDE VARIETY OF BIRDS. THIS ATTRACTIVE BIRDHOUSE IS SUITABLE FOR MOST COMMON SPECIES, INCLUDING BARN OWLS. TO ATTRACT SCREECH OWLS AND OTHER MEMBERS OF THE OWL FAMILY, INCREASE THE HEIGHT OF THE WALLS, TO GIVE A DEPTH 10 TO 12 IN. BELOW A 2½ TO 6 IN. DIAMETER ENTRANCE HOLE.

MATERIALS

1 piece of 52 x 48 x ⅜ in.
plywood
1 piece of 72 x 1 x ½ in.
plywood
1 length 12 in. wide
aluminum self-adhesive
flashing material
Exterior wood glue
Stain and paint
¾ in. molding pins
Screws

WALLS

❶ Cut six 7 x 7 in. wall segments to size from ⅜ in. plywood and mark one face of each (the inside face when the segments are glued together). Stack all six together in a vise, and plane to the same size, leaving all the edges square.

❷ Use a sliding bevel to accurately mark the 60-deg. angle on the edges of each piece and draw lines across the marked face. Bevel the edge of each segment by planing down to the line, taking care not to decrease the width.

❸ Tape the six segments together and stand them on a piece of ½ in. plywood. Check that each pair of sides are equidistant and parallel. Draw along the inside edges to mark out the internal hexagonal shape on the plywood.

❹ Score along any pencil lines that run across the grain, before cutting out the internal base. Make sure you cut along the outside of the lines, otherwise the base will be too small.

❺ Mark out the center point of the entrance hole on one of the segments, and cut the hole using a hole saw held in a drill. The size of the hole should be chosen to suit the species that you are hoping to attract.

Layout of roof panels

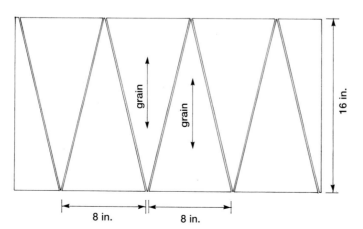

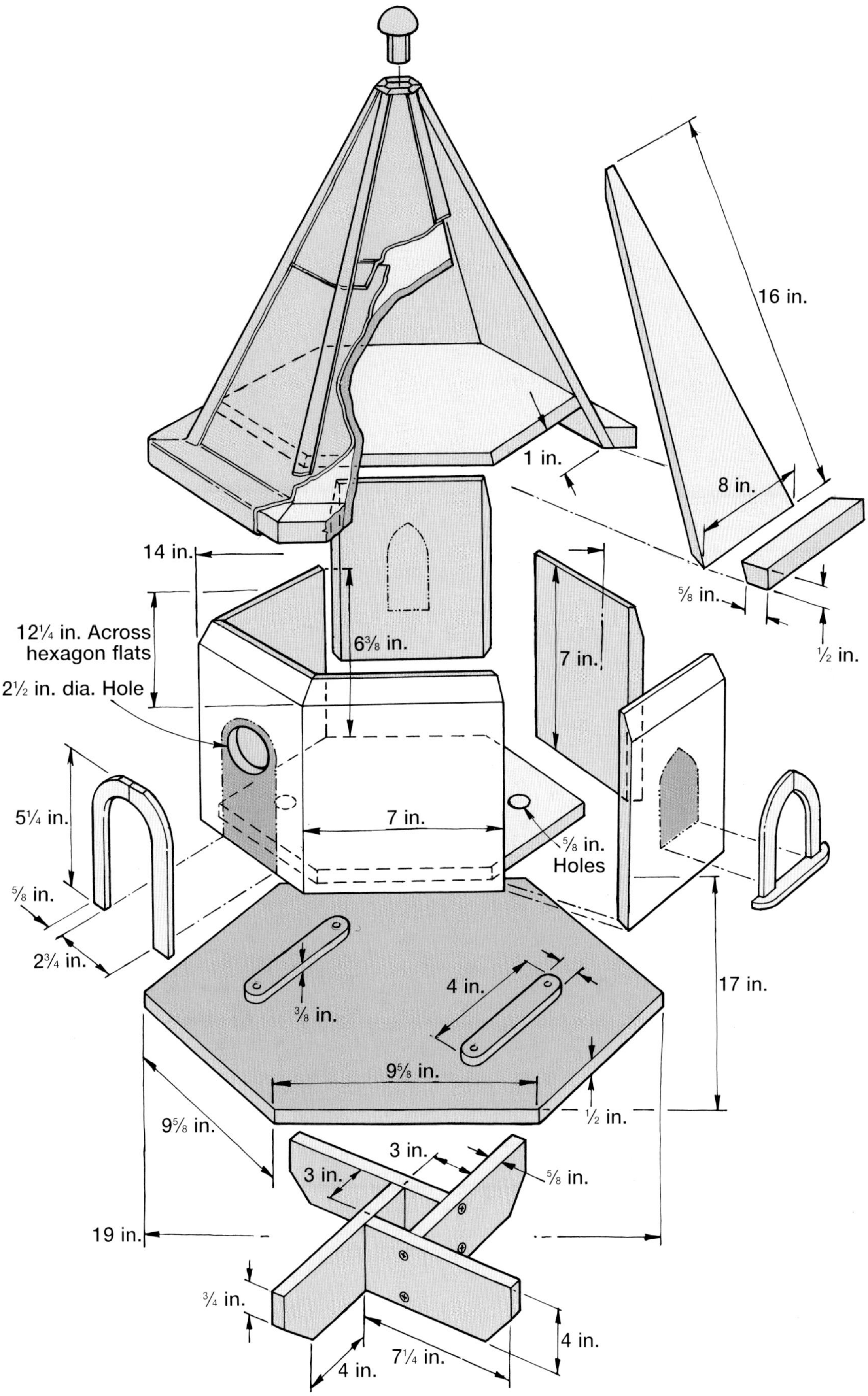
16 in.
1 in.
8 in.
14 in.
⅝ in.
12¼ in. Across
hexagon flats
6⅜ in.
7 in.
½ in.
2½ in. dia. Hole
5¼ in.
7 in.
⅝ in.
Holes
⅝ in.
2¾ in.
4 in.
⅜ in.
17 in.
9⅝ in.
9⅝ in.
½ in.
3 in.
3 in.
⅝ in.
19 in.
¾ in.
4 in.
7¼ in.
4 in.

6 Draw a line ⅛ in. up from the bottom edge on the inside face of each segment. Glue and pin each segment to the base, applying glue to each edge joint in turn. Align the bottom edges of the base with the line drawn on the segments, to leave a lip. Use a piece of string as a tourniquet, to pull the edge joints together and secure with tape until dry.

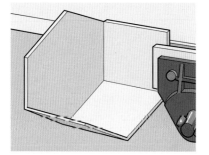

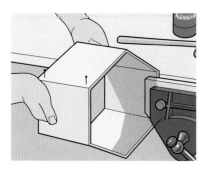

R O O F

7 Draw the six triangular roof segments (base 8 in. x height 16 in.) on a piece of plywood with the grain running along their length and the wide and narrow ends alternated. Leave a gap of ⅛ in. between each to allow for the width of the saw blade. Score across the grain along the long edges before cutting out.

8 Cut out each segment and mark one face of each (this will be the inside face when the segments are glued together). Stack all six together in a vise, and plane all to the same size with all the edges square.

9 On the abutting edges of two of the segments mark a 60-deg. angle and join them with a line drawn

across the inside face. The actual finished angle will be slightly more than 60 deg. but this will provide a good guide to work to.

10 Bevel the edges of the two segments by planing down to the line, taking care not to decrease the width of each piece. Check and adjust the angle by lightly planing until their faces mate along their full length when their bases are set at an angle of 120 deg. (angle at which the walls meet). Set a bevel gauge to the finished edge angle and mark and plane the remaining segment edges to this angle. Mark this angle (x) on a piece of scrap wood for reference when cutting the edge bead (step 14).

11 Tape the roof segments together and set the sliding bevel to the roof pitch angle. Mark this angle (y) on a piece of scrap wood for reference when cutting edge bead (step 14).

12 Glue and pin the segments together, applying glue to each edge joint in turn and taping them until the glue has dried.

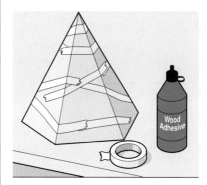

13 Mark out and cut a hexagon from a piece of ⅜ in. plywood, ¾ in. smaller than the base of the roof. Mark out and plane the edges of the hexagonal piece to the roof angle. When the roof is dry, check that the hexagon fits into it, leaving at least a 1 in. lip from the bottom edge,

before gluing it in place. Check that it lies parallel to the bottom edge on all sides. When dry, plane the edge joints flush with the face of each roof segment.

14 Plane one edge of a length of 1 x ½ in. batten to match the roof pitch angle (y) (see step 11). Mark out the length of the bottom edge of one roof segment along the angled edge of the batten. Set the sliding bevel to the roof segment edge angle (x) and mark the angle at each end of the length. Mark out six pieces in this way, but cut them all slightly over length. Use a sharp chisel or sanding disk to trim end angle to allow the end of each bead to mate when fitted around the bottom edge of the roof. Glue and clamp each piece in place until dry.

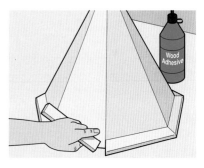

15 Trim the beads to meet equally around the roof and trim and round over the point at the top.

16 Hold the completed wall section firmly in a vise or clamped to a bench. Plane the top edge of each wall segment to match the roof pitch angle (y) (see step 11).

WINDOW AND DOOR FRAMES

17 On thin plywood, mark out the arched door and window frames and score the curved edges. Mark out the position of each piece on the walls.

18 Cut out each piece and glue in position on the walls. Cut two lengths of bead to form the windowsills. Round over each end and glue each in place.

BASEBOARD

19 Mark out and cut the hexagonal baseboard (17 in. measured across the flats) from ½ in. plywood and plane each edge straight and square.

20 Position the wall section on the base, and draw round it. Cut two 4 x 1 x ⅜ in. spacers and glue and screw them to the baseboard within the wall area (the spacers lift the house to prevent rainwater being trapped beneath).

21 Mark out and cut the four support brackets from a piece of ¾ in. wood. Screw the four pieces together and position them on the underside of the baseboard. Drill through the baseboard and glue and screw the battens to the underside.

ROOF COVERING

22 For the roof covering we have used bitumen-backed simulated-lead-finish aluminum foil. This is a self-adhesive material available from builders' merchants and similar stores. Take care when rolling out the foil to avoid creasing it too much.

23 Draw out and cut paper patterns for the top and bottom pieces of foil, leaving adequate margins for trimming. Using a craft knife and steel straight edge, cut out the six lower pieces. Warm the bitumen gently with a hot-air gun, before applying the foil to the roof. Position the piece carefully and trim off the edges along the joint lines. Press the bottom edges to the back of the beads and wrap it over and under them. Trim it to the inside edge of the roof. Repeat this with each lower piece, before cutting and repeating the procedure for the top pieces. Leave an overlap of 3/16 in. between the top and lower pieces. Cut six ¼ in. strips and fold and stick them over the edge joints. Cut a small hexagonal patch and lay this over the top and fold it down over the rounded point.

FINISHING TOUCHES

After filling any defects and recessed pin and screw heads with epoxy filler, sand all surfaces smooth. Paint the outer walls with exterior paint. The climbing plants and foliage are painted on using acrylic paint.

Paint both the baseboard and support battens with a suitable non-toxic exterior-finish varnish or stain.

Screw the house in place over the spacers ready for mounting on a square or round section post.

DUCK HOUSE

DUCKS TEND TO MAKE THEIR NESTS WHEREVER THEY CAN, IN THE OPEN, AMONG REEDS, AND IN HOLLOW BANKS. SOME SPECIES SUCH AS WOOD DUCKS, BARROW'S GOLDENEYE, BUFFLEHEAD, AND BOTH COMMON AND HOODED MERGANSERS, ARE KNOWN TO EVEN NEST IN TREES. THEREFORE MOST DUCKS WILL FAVOR A PURPOSE-BUILT DUCK HOUSE. HOWEVER, THEY DO LIKE TO BE ABLE TO SEE OUT WHEN SITTING ON THE NEST, HENCE THE LOUVERED ROOF DESIGN ON OUR EXAMPLE. ONE OTHER FEATURE IS A SIMPLE PORCH, TO GIVE THE DUCK AND HER YOUNG SOME PROTECTION FROM WIND AND WEATHER BLOWING DIRECTLY INTO THE ENTRANCE HOLE.

THE SIZE OF THE HOUSE SHOWN IS INTENDED FOR MEDIUM-SIZE DUCKS SUCH AS MALLARDS AND SHELDUCK, AND WITH THE ENTRANCE REDUCED TO 4 IN. AND RAISED HIGHER ABOVE THE FLOOR, GOLDENEYE AND WOOD DUCKS.

WALLS AND ROOF

1 Draw out the front and rear walls on ¾ in. plywood. Score across the grain and use a jigsaw to cut around the undercuts.

In case there is any variation in lumber sizes between suppliers, check that the board to be used will be a snug fit in the undercut and adjust accordingly. Take care to cut the edges straight, and square the edges with a plane or rasp. Paint the edges of plywood thoroughly to seal them.

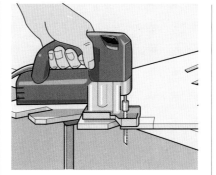

MATERIALS

1 piece of 48 x 36 x ¾ in. plywood
1 piece of 96 x 6 x ¾ in. timber
1 piece of 72 x 6 x ¾ in. timber
1 piece of 30 x 4 x ¾ in. timber
1 piece of 24 x ½ x ¾ in. timber
1 piece of 84 x 1 ¾ x 1 ¾ in. timber
1 piece of 72 x 2 ½ x ¾ in. timber
1 piece of 120 x ½ in. half-round bead
Exterior wood glue
Screws
¾ in. molding pins
Paint

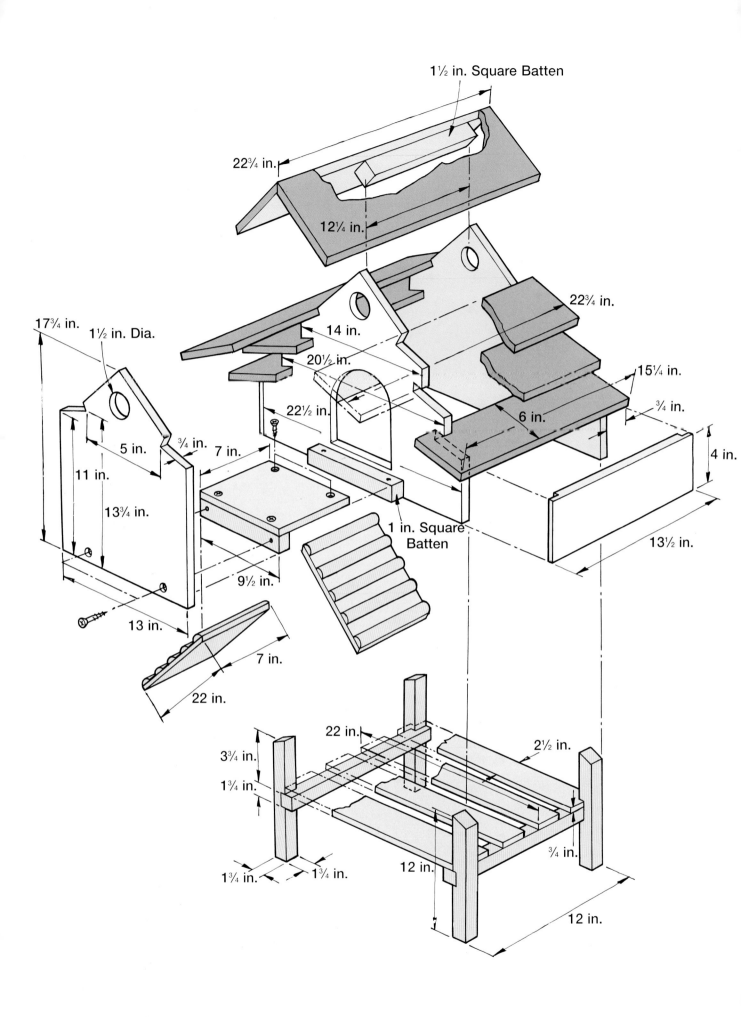

1½ in. Square Batten

22¾ in.

12¼ in.

22¾ in.

17¾ in.

1½ in. Dia.

14 in.

15¼ in.

20½ in.

22½ in.

¾ in.

6 in.

4 in.

5 in.

¾ in.

7 in.

11 in.

13¾ in.

1 in. Square
Batten

13½ in.

9½ in.

13 in.

7 in.

22 in.

22 in.

2½ in.

3¾ in.

1¾ in.

¾ in.

1¾ in.

1¾ in.

1¾ in.

12 in.

12 in.

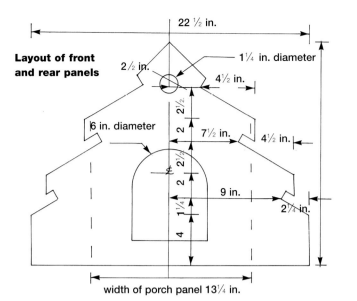

Layout of front and rear panels

22 1/2 in.

2 1/2 in.

1 1/4 in. diameter

4 1/2 in.

6 in. diameter

2 1/2

2

7 1/2 in.

4 1/2 in.

2 1/2

2

9 in.

1 1/4

2 3/4 in.

4

width of porch panel 13 1/4 in.

2 Draw out the shape of the entrance hole on one panel. Score around the arch and drill a 3/8 in. hole through the waste. Insert the jigsaw through the hole and cut on the waste side of the scored line. Cut a 1 1/2 in. hole at the top of each panel.

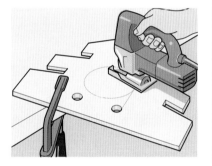

3 Cut the two end boards from 4 x 3/4 in. material to a length of 13 1/2 in. and mark out a 3/4 x 3/8 in. rebate on each end.

4 Score across the rebate line on the face of the boards, and cut in both directions with a hacksaw.

5 Counterbore the screw holes to sink the screw heads and screw the end boards to the front and rear panels aligning the bottom with the bottom edges of the panels.

6 Plane the excess wood away from the top of the board, leaving a beveled edge following the angle of the roof slat.

SLATTED ROOF

7 Cut four 6 x 3/4 in. roof slats to a length of 22 3/4 in. and set out the screw positions and counterbore the holes. Screw and glue the top two slats to the end panels leaving a 3/4 in. overhang at the rear.

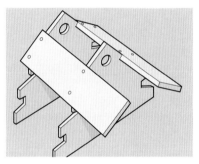

8 Cut a further four slats to a length of 15 1/4 in. and set out the screw positions and counterbore the holes. Screw these boards to the end panels, leaving the same overhang at the back.

9 Cut a third panel from 3/4 in. plywood, similar to the other two but only 13 in. wide. Drill the 1 1/2 in. hole as for previously cut panels.

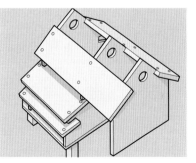

10 Cut three 7 in. wide pieces from 3/4 in. plywood, one x 9 1/2 in. and two x 22 in. long. Cut two 9 1/2 in. lengths of 1 x 1 in. batten, and screw one to the face of the panel, 1 in. below the entrance hole, and the other at a matching height on the rear face of the narrow panel. Screw the shorter of the 7 in. panels between the two battens. Screw the top slats onto the angled shoulders of the narrower panel.

11 Plane one edge of the remaining slats to an angle of 45 deg. Screw these together along the beveled edges. Cut a 1 1/2 x 1 1/2 in. square batten to fit between the two main end panels. Screw and glue the batten into the roof angle to position the ends of the lift-off section in line with the lower slats.

RAISED FLOOR

12 Cut four lengths of 1 3/4 x 1 3/4 in. lumber 12 in. long. Set a sliding bevel to the internal angle between the end board and the lower slat, and cut one end of each leg to this angle. When assembled the legs support the duck house with the underside of the lower slats resting on the beveled end. From the highest edge of the leg, measure down 3 3/4 in. and draw a line across that face. Measure down a further 1 3/4 in. for the halving joint, and set out its depth of 5/8 in. on either side. Cut the halvings by making a series of cuts through the wood and chisel out the waste.

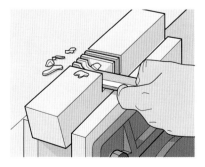

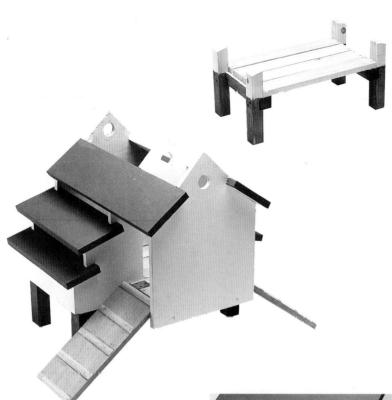

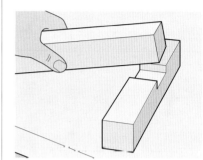

13 Cut the two cross rails to length to fit across the inside width of the house. Screw and glue the rails into the halvings. Cut four 2½ x ¾ in. slats 22 in. long (check that they are a clearance fit inside the house). Screw and glue these to the cross rails leaving equal gaps between them.

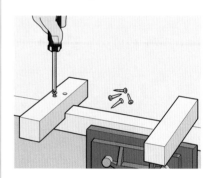

FINISHING TOUCHES

After filling any defects and recessed pin and screw heads with epoxy filler, sand all surfaces smooth. Finish the outer walls and roof with non-toxic stain or varnish, or paint, and protect the lower parts of the legs with a water-based preservative.

14 The two entrance ramps are fitted by hinging them with a pair of back flap hinges (ideally brass), screwed to the underside of the ramp and the entrance step. Pin five equally spaced lengths of half-round bead across the ramp, sinking the pin heads so that they cannot work up above the surface and cause injury to the ducks.

PURPLE MARTIN CONDO

PURPLE MARTINS ARE ONE OF THE FEW BIRDS THAT PREFER TO LIVE IN COLONIES.

MADE OF THICK WOOD AND PLYWOOD FOR GOOD INSULATION, THE HOUSE SHOULD

BE MOUNTED AT A HEIGHT OF BETWEEN 12 AND 20 FEET ABOVE GROUND. HOWEVER, NESTS

MUST BE CHECKED AT LEAST WEEKLY FOR THE REMOVAL OF MITES.

AS THE HOUSE IS FAIRLY HEAVY, OUR DESIGN ALLOWS FOR JUST THE COMPARTMENT

SECTION TO BE LOWERED, LEAVING THE ROOF FIXED TO THE POLE. TO MAKE THIS EASIER, A

PULLEY SYSTEM CAN BE EMPLOYED WITH A PULLEY FITTED INTO THE OPEN CENTER SECTION.

THE IDEAL COMPARTMENT SIZE FOR PURPLE MARTINS IS AROUND 6 X 6 IN.

MATERIALS

2 pieces of 132 x 6 x ¾ in.
timber

1 piece of 48 x 3 x ¾ in.
timber

1 piece of 36 x 2 x ¾ in.
timber

1 piece of 60 x 36 x ½ in.
plywood

1 piece of 4 x 2 sawn
timber (x height of post
required)

1 piece of 60 x 1 ½ x 1 ½ in.
timber

Exterior wood glue

Paint

Screws

(Pulley, rope, and cleat if
hoist required)

1 Cut two 19 in. lengths of 6 x ¾ in. wood and mark the inside face. Divide the inside faces into two and mark out a ¾ x ⅜ in. housing on each. On each end mark out a ¾ x ⅜ in. rebate.

2 Cut two 20¼ in. lengths of 6 x ¾ in. wood and mark the inside face. Divide the inside face into three and mark out two ¾ x ⅜ in. housings on each. Equidistant between each halving, mark the center of the entrance holes.

3 Score the rebate lines and cut in both directions with a backsaw. Score and cut across the halving lines. Remove waste with a chisel.

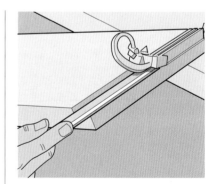

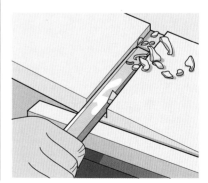

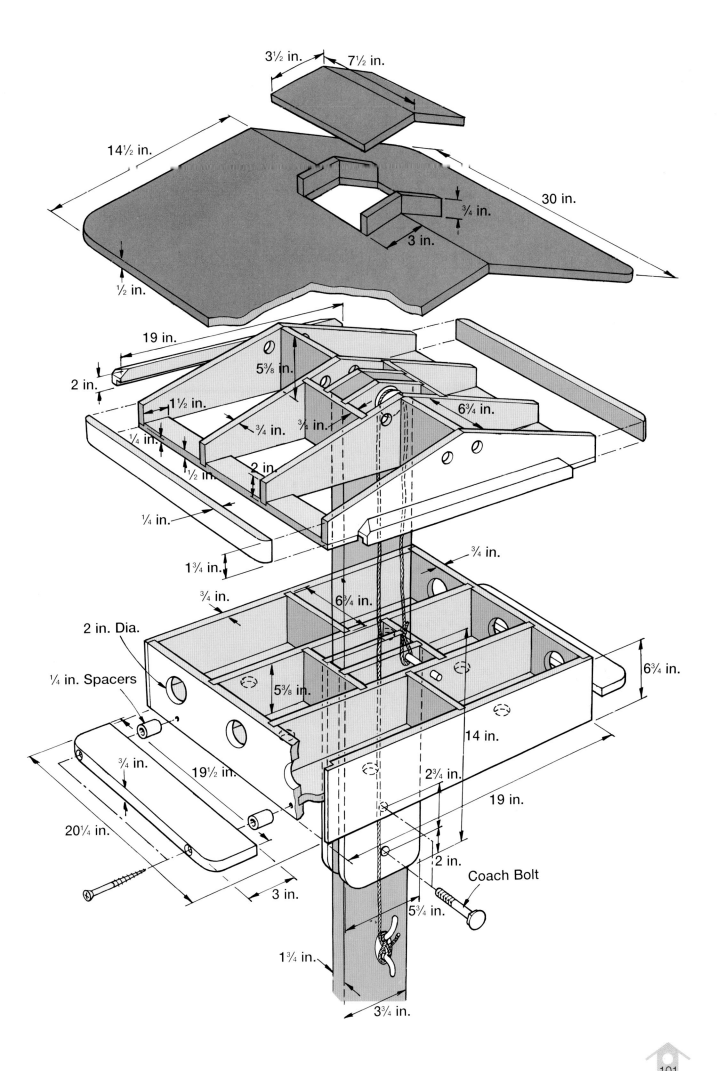

4 Using a 2 in. diameter hole saw, drill the entrance holes from both sides.

5 Along the bottom edge on the inside face of each piece cut a $\frac{5}{8} \times \frac{3}{8}$ in. rebate.

6 Cut two $18\frac{1}{4}$ in. lengths of $5\frac{3}{8} \times \frac{3}{4}$ in. wood. Divide one face on each into two and mark out a $\frac{3}{4} \times \frac{3}{8}$ in. housing on each. Divide the other face into three and mark out two $\frac{3}{4} \times \frac{3}{8}$ in. housings on each.

7 Temporarily clamp the six pieces together to form a square with the divisions in place.

8 Cut four $6\frac{3}{4}$ in. lengths of $5\frac{3}{8} \times \frac{3}{4}$ in. wood. On two of them, mark out two housings $\frac{1}{2} \times \frac{3}{8}$ in. on one face, 1 in. either side of the center line.

9 Reassemble the compartments, gluing the division joints and gluing and screwing the rebated corner joints.

10 Cut two $19\frac{1}{2}$ in. lengths of $3 \times \frac{3}{4}$ in. wood. Round two corners on one edge to a radius of $\frac{3}{4}$ in., and drill two $\frac{1}{4}$ in. diameter holes through the full width, 3 in. inward from each end.

11 Cut two $9\frac{1}{4} \times 20\frac{1}{4} \times \frac{1}{2}$ in. plywood floor panels, plane the edges square, and check that they fit into the bottom rebate. Along the meeting edge form a cutout around the center vent and post hole and the two mounting plate housings. Glue and screw the panels into the rebates and to the bottom edges of the compartment divisions.

12 Cut two $5\frac{3}{4} \times 14 \times \frac{1}{2}$ in. plywood plates and form the stepped side edges to allow the plate to fit up into the housings. Glue the two plates into position.

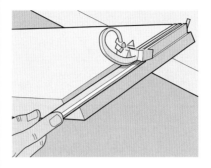

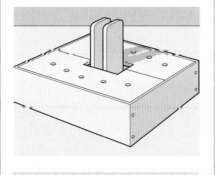

ROOF

13 Cut four 22 in. lengths of $6 \times \frac{3}{4}$ in. wood. Mark out the roof angle on each, taking it from the center of the top edge to a point 4 in. down the end and cut along each piece. Clamp them together in a vise, and plane them all to the same size, leaving the edges square. Either side of the center housing on each rafter, drill a $\frac{1}{2}$ in. diameter ventilation hole.

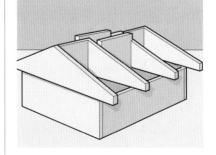

14 Divide one face on each into two and mark out a $\frac{3}{4} \times \frac{3}{8}$ in. housing on each. Divide the other face on two pieces into three and mark out two $\frac{3}{4} \times \frac{3}{8}$ in. housings on each. Cut the housings as before.

15 Cut four $6\frac{3}{4}$ in. lengths of $5\frac{3}{8} \times \frac{3}{4}$ in. wood. Clamp the frame together, and mark the beveled top edges of the short divisions. Cut and plane these to the correct height and angle. Glue and clamp the frame together, checking that the rafters are parallel. Between each housing drill a $\frac{1}{2}$ in. hole.

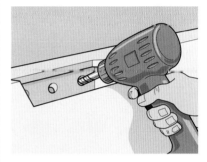

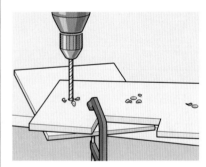

16 Cut $1\frac{1}{2} \times \frac{1}{4}$ in. rebates on the underside of each end of each rafter. Join the ends by gluing and screwing a $1\frac{1}{2} \times \frac{1}{2}$ in. batten into the rebates, checking that the rafters remain parallel to each other. Glue and pin a $1\frac{3}{4} \times \frac{1}{4}$ in. batten across the ends of the rafters and the edge of the bottom batten (this will leave a narrow ventilation gap between the top edge of the batten and the underside of the roof).

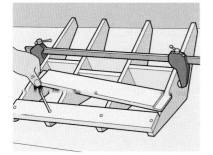

17 Cut the roof from two pieces of ½ in. plywood, leaving an overhang of ½ in. at the front and 2 in. at either end. Use a sliding bevel to mark out the miter angle on both ends of each piece, and draw a line between the points. Plane a bevel along the edges, down to the line. Cut out the center section along the meeting edges for the raised vent and round the bottom corners of each piece. Glue and screw the roof onto the rafters.

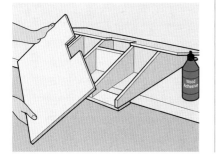

18 Cut four 3 x ½ x ¾ in. blocks and miter one end of each. Glue and pin the blocks to the roof at either end of the vent opening. Cut the two 7¼ x 3½ x ½ in. plywood vent panels and plane a miter along the one edge of each. Glue and pin the panels to the spacer blocks.

19 Cut two 19 x 2 x ¾ in. battens and plane a bevel along one edge on each. Glue and pin these to the end of roof ends, to overlap the edge by ⅝ in.

20 After filling any defects and recessed pin and screw heads with epoxy filler, sand all surfaces. Paint the roof with masonry paint.

21 Sand the two side perches, and prime and paint. Insert two 4¼ in. coach screws through the holes and fit ¼ in. spacers over the threads. Drill fine pilot holes in the sides of the house and screw the perches to it.

FINISHING TOUCHES

The mounting post or top section of the mounting post should be a snug fit into the post hole. Miter the top of the post to fit into the ventilation cap. When erected, the roof section can be screwed to the roof, allowing the bottom section of the birdhouse to slide down the post for cleaning. The two plates are drilled to take a pair of coach bolts for locking the bottom section against the roof.

For ease of use, a simple pulley system can be fitted to allow the bottom section to be lowered safely.

Mounting plates

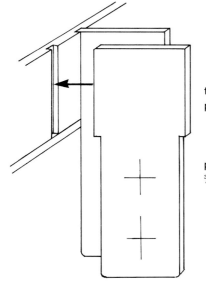

two x 14 x 5¾ x ½ in. plywood plates

plates cut to fit into ⅜ in. rebates

DOVECOTE

A HEXAGONAL DOVECOTE WITH ITS SNOW-WHITE DOVES INTRODUCES ELEGANCE AND GRACE TO THE TRADITIONAL COUNTRY GARDEN.

ATTRACTIVE YET PRACTICAL, OUR LIFT-OFF DESIGN ALLOWS THE DOVECOTE TO BE QUICKLY

DISASSEMBLED FOR EASY CLEANING AND HAS ROOM FOR SIX MATING PAIRS.

COTE SIDES

1 Draw out a template of one of the side segments full size on a sheet of paper, taking the dimensions from our drawing. Start by drawing a center line on the sheet and measure half the width of the segment on either side of the line. The side angle will then be equal on either edge.

2 Cut out the template carefully. Set the template against the straight edges of a sheet of ⅜ in. plywood and mark out the six segments from it.

3 After scoring across the grain, cut out each segment and mark one face of each (this will be the inside face when the segments are glued together). Stack all six together with one end held in a vise and the other clamped together and supported from underneath (this is to prevent the sheets dropping as they are being planed). Plane all to the same size, leaving the edges square.

Layout of roof panels

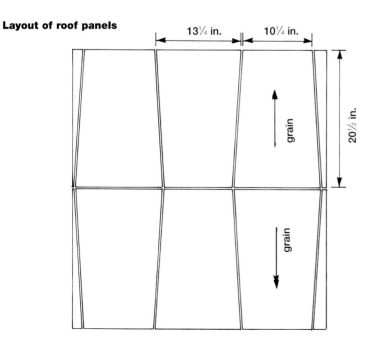

13¼ in.   10¼ in.

grain

grain

20½ in.

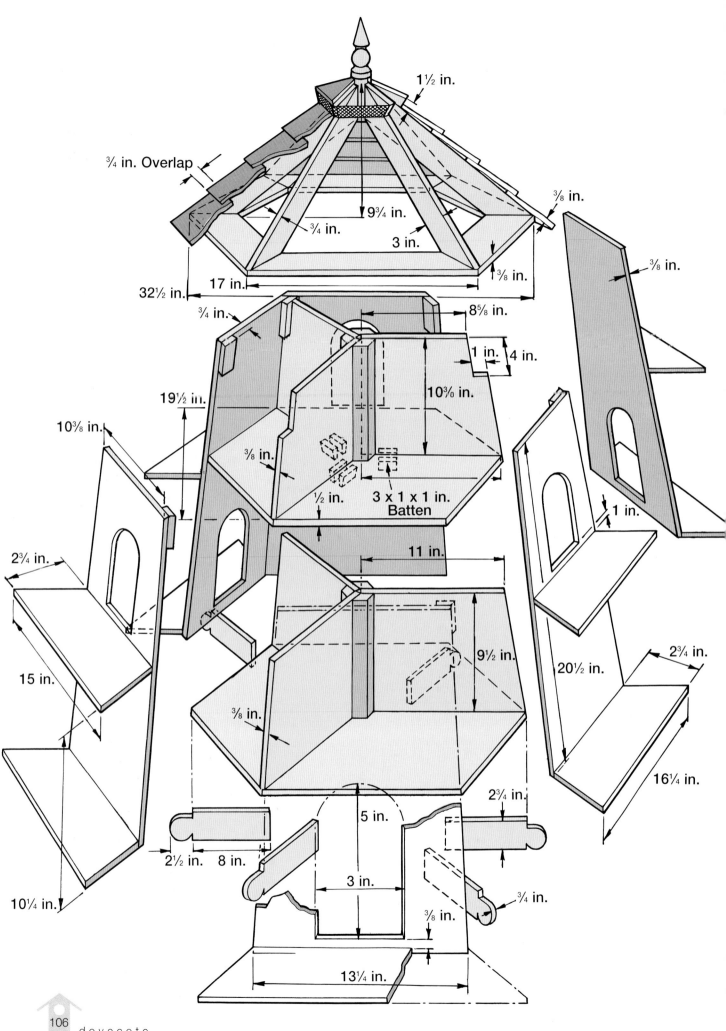

1½ in.

¾ in. Overlap

3⁄8 in.

9¾ in.

¾ in.

3 in.

3⁄8 in.

3⁄8 in.

32½ in.

17 in.

8⅝ in.

¾ in.

1 in.

4 in.

10⅜ in.

19½ in.

3⁄8 in.

10⅜ in.

½ in.

3 x 1 x 1 in.
Batten

11 in.

1 in.

2¾ in.

9½ in.

20½ in.

2¾ in.

15 in.

3⁄8 in.

2¾ in.

16¼ in.

5 in.

2½ in.   8 in.

3 in.

3⁄8 in.

¾ in.

10¼ in.

13¼ in.

4 To find the angle of the side panel edge joints, take two segments and mark the abutting vertical edges. On both ends of the piece draw an angle of 60 deg. toward the marked face. Join the lower points with a line drawn parallel to the edge.

5 Bevel the edges of the segment by planing down to the line, taking care not to decrease the width of the side. Check and adjust the angle by lightly planing until their faces mate along their full length when their bases are set at an angle of 120 deg. Set a bevel gauge to the finished edge angle and mark and plane the remaining segment edges to this angle.

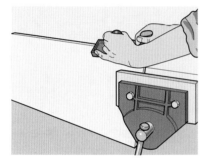

6 Glue and pin each segment together, applying glue to each edge joint in turn and taping them until the glue dries. Check that each facing pair of segments are parallel and that the diagonal dimensions across the corners of the hexagon are equal.

7 On the face of each segment draw a center line from top to bottom. Mark out the position and shape of the entrance holes, centering them on this line. Score across the grain, before cutting the holes out with a jigsaw. Finish the edges of the entrance holes with a rasp and sanding with abrasive paper wrapped over a square block for the straight edges and a curved block for the arched tops.

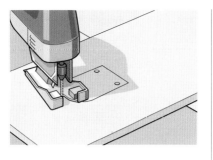

8 Glue and pin the segments together in pairs, checking before joining the three pairs together, to complete the hexagon. Use strap clamps to hold the completed cote while the glue dries.

9 Cut three lengths of ¾ x 2 x 24 in. batten. The narrow edges of these are to be planed to an angle of 60 deg. Mark the angle on both ends of the batten, on opposite faces (to form a rhombus). Draw, or scribe with a marking gauge, a line along the batten faces, parallel to the edges. Hold the batten in the vise and plane down to the line. Cut a 2 x 1½ in. length from the top of each and glue and clamp these blocks into the angle at the top of the vertical joints. When dry, plane the vertical joints flush.

10 With the cote standing on a flat surface, use a sliding bevel to take the vertical angle (x) of the sides.

11 Cut 12 17 in. lengths of 3 x ¾ in. wood. Transfer the vertical side angle to both ends of each piece and connect the lower points with a pencil or scribed line.

12 Hold the wood securely in a vise and plane a bevel down to the line.

13 Set the sliding bevel to an angle of 60 deg. and transfer it to one end of each length of wood, splaying out from the beveled edge.

14 Cut the angle on one end of two of the lengths and check the miter against the base of the tapered sides. Lightly plane the miter faces to close any gaps. Hold the piece of wood, with the bevel edge against the base of the side, and mark the length. Set the sliding bevel to the adjusted angle (if necessary), and mark out and cut the angle. Glue and screw the lengths around the base of the dovecote and drill and screw through the side of the wood into the end of the mating board. This is to pull the joints tight. If any are cut too short, lightly plane the beveled edge.

15 Draw a line around the dovecote, 1 in. below the upper entrance holes. To fit the high perch, position the top edge of the wood against the line as before.

16 As the perch widths may vary, choose the narrowest width, and draw a line equidistant from the side of the cote along the top face of each section (these lines should all meet up at each end). Plane the front edges of the perches to the line.

NESTING COMPARTMENTS

17 On the inside of the dovecote, measure the width of the sides at a point ½ in. below the upper entrance holes. Use this dimension to set out the hexagonal floor of the upper compartment on a piece of ½ in. plywood. In a similar manner, measure around the base at a point 1¼ in. above the bottom edge and set out the lower hexagonal floor. Score across the grain and cut out both floors. Check that both floors fit at the correct level, leaving a small clearance on each each side (about ⅛ in. all round).

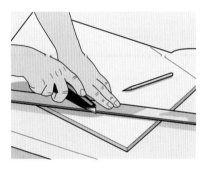

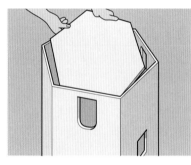

18 Using the batten cut in step 9, cut three lengths of 10⅜ in. and three lengths of 9½ in. Set the sliding bevel against the angle on the inside of the vertical joints. On both floors set out the position of the three compartment divisions. On ⅜ in. plywood draw out the six divisions, taking the base dimensions from the floors and using the sliding bevel to set out the angled edge. Score across the grain and cut out the divisions. On the upper floor division, cut the corner notch to fit over the angled blocks glued to the inside of the cote (the cote actually rests on these).

19 Glue and screw a length of the angled batten to the vertical edge of each division, on the same face. Glue and pin the two sets of matching divisions together, and check that they fit correctly into the cote. Glue and pin both to their respective floor. On the underside of the upper floor, glue three sets of short battens (3 x I x I In.) to locate at the top edge of the lower divisions.

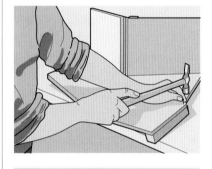

ROOF

20 Cut the six rafters from a piece of 3 x ¾ in. wood, to a length of 23 in. Cut an angle of 45 deg. at both ends.

21 Glue two pieces of 2 x 1 x 6 in. wood together and trim the ends square. Draw an equal-sided hexagon at both ends and draw a line between the points on the face of the wood. Hold the piece in a vise and plane the beveled faces to the line.

22 Hold the center post in the vise, and screw each rafter to it, countersinking the screw heads.

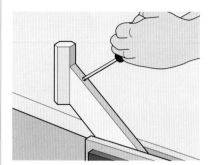

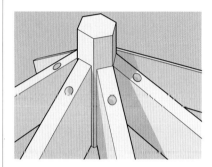

23 Stand the assembled rafters centrally on the cote, with each rafter sitting over a corner joint. Mark the point where the apex of the corner joints touch the rafters. Mark out and cut a notch (bird's mouth) at this point on each rafter, to allow the roof to sit over the sides of the cote. Place the roof back on the cote and measure the distance from the cote sides to the end of the rafters (dimension a). Draw a line around the cote level with the bottom of the rafters (b).

SOFFIT BOARD

24 Cut six pieces of ⅜ in. plywood, 17 in. long x (a + 1 in.). Set the sliding bevel to 60 deg. and transfer the angle to one end of each length of wood.

25 Cut the angle, on one end of each length. Measure the width of the cote side on the rafter line (b), and transfer this to each piece. Mark out and cut the opposite ends to the same angle. With the rafters sitting on the cote, check that the soffit boards touch the sides of the cote and that the miter faces meet. If any lengths are short, leaving the joint open, lightly plane the back edge. Glue and pin the lengths to the rafters.

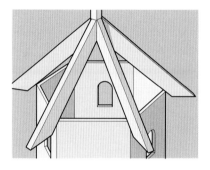

26 To allow the roof boards to lie flat on the rafters, it is necessary to plane a bevel on either side of the top edge. Draw a center line down the edge of each rafter, and plane the bevel away to each side. Check the bevel between each pair of rafters by laying a straight edge across them. Plane the front top edge of the soffit board to lie flush with the beveled edges of the rafters and plane the front edge of each section of soffit board to an equal width, leaving a minimum edge thickness of $\frac{1}{4}$ in.

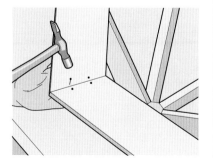

ROOF BOARDS

27 Cut six 18 in. lengths of $4\frac{1}{2}$ x $\frac{3}{8}$ in. plywood. Set the sliding bevel to the angle between the front edge of the soffit board and the center line of the rafters. Transfer this angle to both a piece of scrap wood for future reference and to the end of one roof board. Measure the distance between the very tip of the rafters and add 1 in. Mark this length off along the front edge of the roof board. Mark out the end angle as before and cut the two angles.

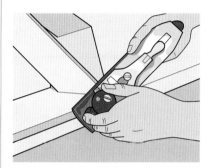

28 Pin the board temporarily to the rafters, aligning the miter faces on the rafter center line, and the front edge parallel to the soffit board. Cut a second board in the same way and lay it next to the first. The miter faces need to be slightly beveled for them to meet. Mark approximately half of the vertical angle on the edge of each board, and plane one miter face to it. Repeat this on the second face, lightly planing until the two faces meet. Set the sliding bevel to this angle and transfer it to a piece of scrap wood for future reference.

29 Glue and pin the bottom boards to the rafters before starting the next row. When cutting each of the remaining roof boards, mark both angles in a similar manner using the reference angles to mark out each board end, but cutting the angle in both directions in one cut. Slight adjustment can then be made by planing. Allow an overlap of at least $\frac{3}{4}$ in. between each board, and plane a bevel on the top edge of each board as for the soffit board, to allow the next board to lie on a flat surface.

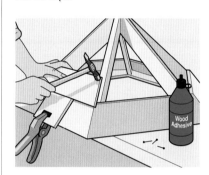

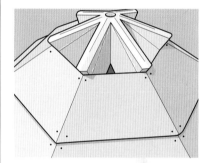

30 Cut six tapered ¾ in. thick blocks, 1½ in. high at one end. Their length is taken from the remaining length of rafter after the roof boards are fitted. Before gluing the blocks in position it is necessary to remove the bevel from the rafters over this length. This can be done with a sharp chisel. Glue the blocks in place. Cut the center post ⅜ in. higher than the vent blocks and plane a double bevel (as on the rafters) to run into the post.

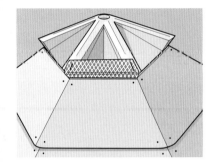

31 Staple fine-gauge aluminum mesh over the front of the vent before cutting and fitting the final row of roof boards.

FINIALS

32 The top finial can be turned on a lathe, leaving a ¾ in. spigot for gluing into a hole drilled in the center of the post. Alternatively a turned wooden door knob can be used, screwed in place with a double-ended screw (handrail screw).

MOUNTING

33 Our dovecote was mounted on a 6 in. square post. The top section was cut down to 4 in. to locate in a metal cup (the type used for mounting fence posts on concrete or paving). The cup is bolted through the floor of the lower compartments. As a decorative feature, six false beams are screwed to the underside of the floor at each corner of the hexagon. Cut these – 8½ in. long – from 3 x ¾ in. wood. Draw the circular detail, and cut with the jigsaw.

FINISHING TOUCHES

After filling any defects and recessed pin and screw heads with epoxy filler, sand all surfaces smooth. The sides of the cote are primed and painted with a non-toxic paint system. The roof can be painted in a similar way, or sealed and primed and finished with an exterior masonry paint.

THE OLD
SCHOOLHOUSE

THE CLAPBOARD EFFECT OF THIS HANDSOME, TWO-STORY NESTING BOX IS CREATED

BY CUTTING SHALLOW HORIZONTAL GROOVES WITH A SMALL BACKSAW. THE

SCHOOLHOUSE MIGHT SUIT A WOODPECKER, BUT BEAR IN MIND THAT EXCAVATING A NEST

CAVITY IS AN IMPORTANT PART OF COURTSHIP BEHAVIOR FOR THIS SPECIES, SO MAKE IT

ATTRACTIVE BY FILLING THE BOX WITH WOOD CHIPS TO PROVIDE EXCAVATION MATERIAL.

MATERIALS

1 piece of 39 x 39 x ½ in.
plywood
1 piece of 18 x ½ in.
diameter dowel
1 piece of 10 x ½ x ½ in.
timber
Exterior wood glue
Screws
¾ in. molding pins
Paint

1 Mark out the main parts and cut them roughly. Trim back to the pencil lines with a plane.

2 Draw parallel, horizontal lines in pencil and then cut shallow grooves in the wall pieces with a backsaw, using a scrap strip of wood as a guide, held in place with C-clamps.

3 To cut the main entry hole, clamp the front to the stand with a piece of scrap wood underneath and drill with hole saw.

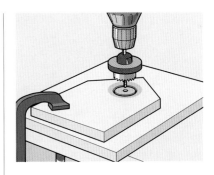

4 Glue and pin all the sides of the birdhouse together using a waterproof glue. Attach the roof, and glue and pin it into position.

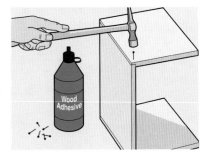

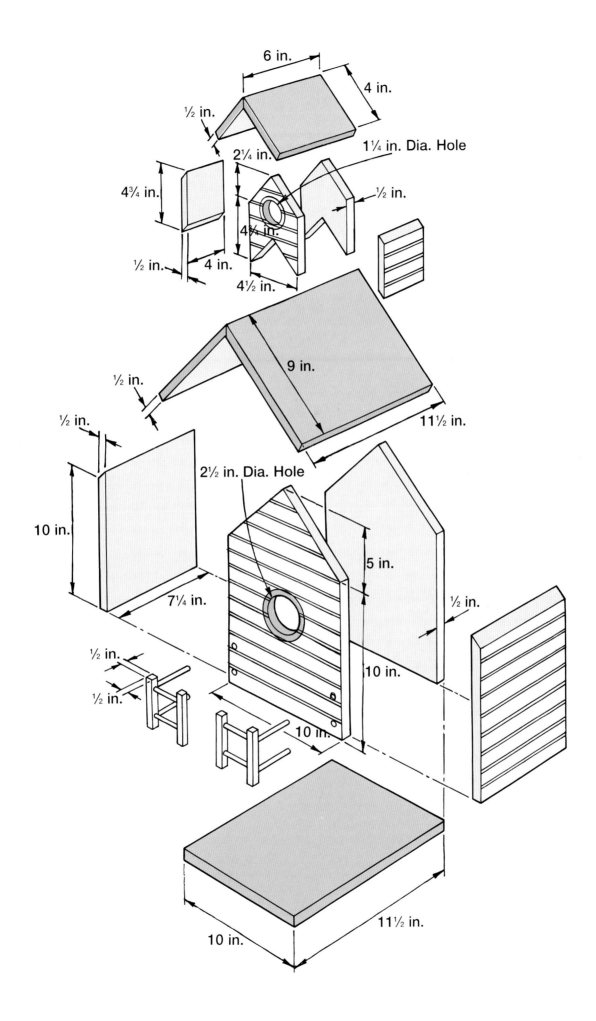

6 in.

4 in.

½ in.

2¼ in.

1¼ in. Dia. Hole

½ in.

4¾ in.

4½ in.

½ in.

4 in.

4½ in.

½ in.

9 in.

½ in.

11½ in.

½ in.

2½ in. Dia. Hole

10 in.

5 in.

½ in.

7¼ in.

10 in.

½ in.

½ in.

10 in.

10 in.

11½ in.

10 in.

5 Lay out the top section of the house and cut the sizes with a backsaw, trimming back to the lines with a plane. Cut the V-shaped section accurately with a backsaw.

6 Drill a smaller entry hole in this section, if required. Glue and pin to assemble.

7 Attach the smaller house on top of the large one. Glue and pin the top house to the lower one from the inside.

8 Using a fine-toothed saw, cut the dowel and the hardwood into the lengths given to make the balustrade. Use a ¼ in. drill to make holes in the uprights to take the dowel.

9 Sand all parts of the house. Assemble the balustrade, gluing and then tapping the doweling into place.

10 Assemble all the parts of the house, using plated screws to withstand outdoor conditions.

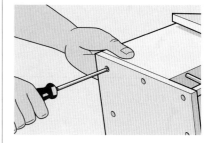

11 Finish the outside by painting with water-based, exterior-grade undercoat, then a flat-finish top coat.

Bird feeder projects

from a sculptured tree feeder

to a timely decorative feature

– bird tables for varied settings

OLD TOOLS

OLD SPADES, FORKS, AND OTHER DISCARDED GARDENING TOOLS CAN

BE TURNED INTO ATTRACTIVE FEEDERS SIMPLY BY HOOKING ON A

SIMPLE BIRD TABLE. FINISH THE OLD TOOL WITH A RUST-INHIBITING PAINT BEFORE SIMPLY

DIGGING IT INTO THE GROUND IN A SUITABLE POSITION IN THE GARDEN. DISCARDED

SCYTHES, PITCHFORKS, AND OTHER FARMING TOOLS CAN BE ADAPTED IN A SIMILAR WAY,

EITHER DUG INTO THE GROUND OR HUNG ON THE BARN OR HOUSE WALL.

MATERIALS

1 piece of 12 x 18 x ⅜ in.
plywood
1 piece of 5 x ¼ in.
diameter dowel
1¾ in. panel pins
Screws
Stain/varnish

1 On ⅜ in. plywood, draw a 10 in. diameter disk around a suitable container or lid. On one edge of the disk mark out a semicircular notch to fit around the tool's shaft.

2 Use a jigsaw to cut the circle out, after scoring along the line with a craft knife. Cut on the waste side of the line. Use abrasive paper with a sanding block to smooth the edges. Cut out the handle notch and finish the edge with abrasive paper wrapped around a piece of 1 in. dowel.

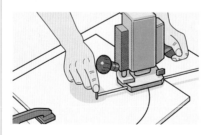

3 Draw out on stiff paper the handle hook from our squared drawing. Each square represents 1 in. Cut the shape out and try the hook on the handle. Sand the edges with abrasive paper wrapped

around a piece of 1 in. dowel. Try it on the handle of your garden fork or spade and adjust the shape to suit.

4 Draw around the template onto ⅜ in. plywood, score along the line, and cut out with a jigsaw. Sand the edges with abrasive paper wrapped around a piece of 1 in. dowel.

5 Drill through the handle hook to take a 5 in. length of ¼ in. diameter dowel, ensuring prior to drilling that the drill size will produce a snug fit. Insert the dowel and drill a fine pilot hole through the edge of the plywood to take a long panel pin to secure it.

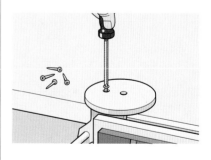

6 Drill two countersunk holes through the disk and screw the handle hook to it.

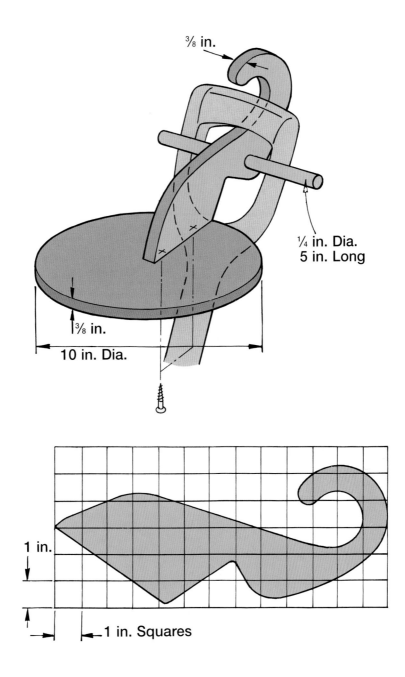

⅜ in.

¼ in. Dia.
5 in. Long

⅜ in.

10 in. Dia.

1 in.

1 in. Squares

FINISHING
TOUCHES

Paint the disk and handle hook with
a water-based stain and/or varnish.

TRIPLE DECKER

THREE TIERS ON THIS TRIPLE-DECKER BIRD TABLE WILL ENSURE THAT IT IS

A HIVE OF ACTIVITY, CONSTANTLY IN USE, BY BOTH SMALL AND LARGE

SPECIES. TO AVOID ANY RISK OF HURTING THE BIRDS, HANG SEED CAKES, FRUIT, AND NUTS

BY TYING THEM THROUGH HOLES DRILLED IN THE FACE OF THE TIERS, RATHER THAN DRIVING

NAILS OR HOOKS INTO THE EDGE.

TRY VARYING THE TYPE OF FOOD ON EACH TIER TO SEE WHICH BIRDS YOU CAN ATTRACT.

BUILD UP A REGISTER OF SPECIES, THE PREFERRED FOODS AND THE SEASONS DURING

WHICH THEY VISIT.

1 On $\frac{3}{8}$ in. plywood, draw three disks of around 20, 10 and 7 in. diameter, by drawing around suitable containers or lids.

2 You can make a simple beam compass from a 12 in. length of 1 x $\frac{1}{4}$ in. batten. At one end of the batten mark a center point. Then measure from this, along the batten, other points at intervals of $\frac{1}{2}$ in. Through the first center point, drill a hole just large enough to grip a pencil. Counting from the pencil end, mark the center points at 3½, 5 and 10 in. At each of these points, drill a fine pilot hole to grip a 1½ in. panel pin.

3 Set the pin to the larger diameter. Dig the pin point lightly into the board and swing the compass to draw a complete circle. Reposition the pin and draw the other two circles. (You can then use the compass for other projects, drilling pin holes at appropriate intervals).

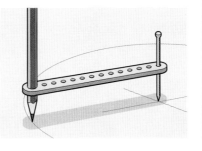

MATERIALS

1 piece of 30 x 24 x $\frac{3}{8}$ in. plywood
1 piece of 30 x 1¼ in. diameter dowel
1 piece 40 x 1 x $\frac{3}{8}$ in. timber
Screws
Paint

Homemade beam compass

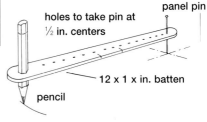

panel pin
holes to take pin at ½ in. centers
12 x 1 x in. batten
pencil

4 Use a jigsaw to cut out the circles, after scoring along the line with a craft knife. Cut on the waste side of the line. Use abrasive paper with a sanding block to smooth the edges. Alternatively, use an electric router fitted with a trammel point for larger diameters, or trammel base for smaller ones. Using the router saves the need for excessive edge finishing.

5 At the center of each circle cut a 1¼ in. diameter hole with a hole saw held in an electric drill.

6 On the larger table, screw four 8⅜ in. lengths of 1 x ⅜ in. batten.

7 With either the jigsaw or router, cut three 4½ in. circles. Cut each of them in half and drill two counter-sunk holes on the center line.

8 The post for the table is made in two parts: a square or round bottom section is drilled to take a 1¼ in. diameter top section. Cut the top section to a length of 30 in., round over the top and mark off the height of each table, starting at the bottom, at 8, 10, and 8 in, and then leave 4 in. at the top.

9 Drill each disk to take the half-round brackets either side of the center hole. Slide the disks over the post to their position, and screw through the bracket into the post.

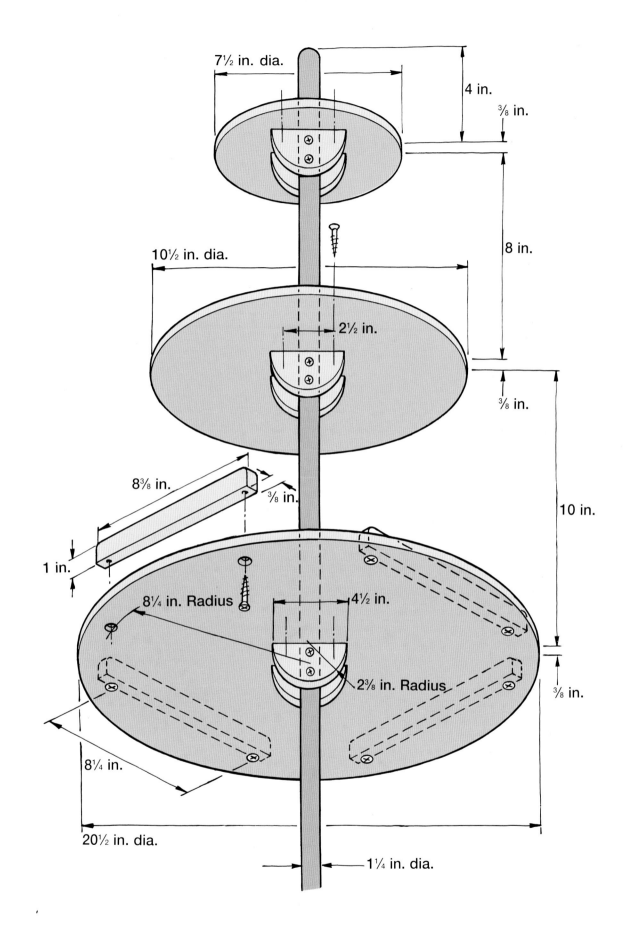

7½ in. dia.

4 in.

⅜ in.

10½ in. dia.

8 in.

2½ in.

⅜ in.

8⅜ in.

⅜ in.

10 in.

1 in.

8¼ in. Radius

4½ in.

2⅜ in. Radius

⅜ in.

8¼ in.

20½ in. dia.

1¼ in. dia.

FLAT TREE
FEEDER

DESIGNED FOR USE ON HARD PAVED AREAS, BALCONIES, AND FLAT ROOFS, THIS ATTRACTIVE TREE FEEDER IS MOUNTED ON A HEAVY PAVING SLAB TO PREVENT IT FROM BEING BLOWN OVER OR ROCKED IN THE WIND. AN ALTERNATIVE BRACKET CAN BE USED IN CONJUNCTION WITH THE SLAB, TO SECURE IT TO A WALL OR FENCE POST.

USE SHALLOW DISHES FOR WATER AND SEED WITH SMALLER CONTAINERS AND MESH FEEDERS FOR NUTS, FRUIT, PET FOODS, AND OTHER TIDBITS TO ATTRACT A WIDE RANGE OF BIRDS. DO REMEMBER TO CLEAN OUT THE CONTAINERS AND DISHES REGULARLY.

MATERIALS

1 48 x 48 in. sheet of ⅜ in.
plywood
1 piece of 7 x 2 x 2 in.
timber
1½ in. thick square or
hexagonal paving slab
A 48 in. length of ½ in.
dowel
1 piece of 15 x 6 x ½ in.
plywood
Six 1 in. x 12 gauge round-
head brass screws
Stain/varnish
Hanging nut feeder and

OTHER TOOLS

Router fitted with straight
bit and trammel bar
Beam compass
(see page 121)

1 Draw the outline of the tree on a 48 x 40 in. sheet of ⅜ in. plywood. Each section of the curved edge is a segment of a regular circle, therefore it can be drawn using a beam compass. Instructions for a simple beam compass can be found in the Triple-decker project on page 121. For this project, counting from the pencil end, mark the center points at 5½, 6, and 8 in. At each of these points, drill a fine pilot hole to grip a 1½ in. panel pin.

3 Set out each center point on the board and set the compass to the appropriate diameter. Dig the pin point lightly into the board and swing the compass to draw a segment of a circle. Repeat this at each center point, crossing the ends of each segment.

4 Set out the trunk of the tree using freehand.

5 Score around the line with a craft knife, before cutting on the waste side (outside) of the line with a jigsaw. Make sure that the plywood is well supported and that the jigsaw cable is held clear of the saw cut. Finish the cut edges by sanding with abrasive paper wrapped over a sanding block.

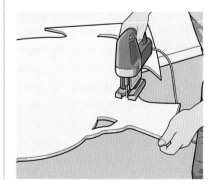

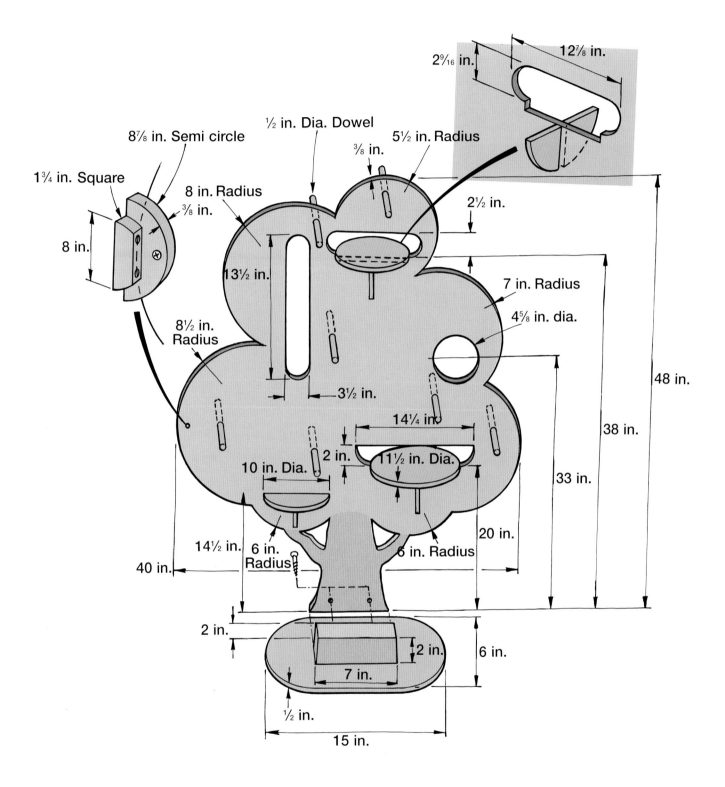

1¾ in. Square

8⅞ in. Semi circle

½ in. Dia. Dowel

⅜ in.

5½ in. Radius

2⁹⁄₁₆ in.

12⅞ in.

8 in. Radius

⅜ in.

2½ in.

8 in.

13½ in.

7 in. Radius

4⅝ in. dia.

8½ in. Radius

48 in.

3½ in.

38 in.

14¼ in.

2 in.

33 in.

10 in. Dia.

11½ in. Dia.

6 in. Radius

14½ in.

6 in. Radius

20 in.

40 in.

2 in.

2 in.

6 in.

7 in.

½ in.

15 in.

FINISHING TOUCHES

After filling any defects with epoxy filler, sand all surfaces smooth. Paint the tree with a water-based stain and/or varnish.

MOUNTING

Cut the 15 x 6 in. base from ½ in. plywood and screw a 7 x 2 x 2 in. piece of wood to it. Drill the base to take two ⅜ in. diameter bolts for fastening to a concrete paving slab. Insure that the bolt heads or nuts do not protrude below the underside of the slab: not only may they cause the tree to move, but they may also damage the roof or balcony surface.

The tree may also be secured to an adjacent wall or fence post. Make up the wall bracket by screwing a half-disk of plywood to a wooden block. Plug and screw the block to the wall or screw it to a post. Attach the tree to the bracket using a bolt and wing nut to allow it to be detached easily.

FOOD AND WATER DISHES

6 Plastic or terracotta dishes for food and water are stood on round bases mounted through the board. The dishes we used were 14 x 1½ in. and 12 x 1¾ in. Mark out a horizontal slot, wide and long enough to slide the dish through. Add to the width ⅜ in. to allow for the base thickness. Drill a hole in the waste area and score around the line at the curved ends. Insert the jigsaw blade through the hole and cut along the waste side of the line.

7 Using the router or a jigsaw, cut a circle with a diameter of 1 in. more than the dish diameter. Similarly, cut a half-circle 2 in. less than the base diameter. Cut the half-circle in half, and glue and screw the two pieces either side of the board. Drill and countersink holes for this, offsetting them by the thickness of the plywood on opposite faces of the board to allow the screws to be inserted for the second piece after the first is fitted.

8 Drill and countersink the base after carefully positioning the hole centers over the brackets. Glue and screw the base onto the brackets.

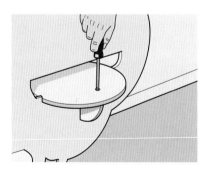

9 Small containers for food or water can be mounted in a similar way as the table but without cutting the slot through the board. Use a flat-sided base with a hole, less than the diameter of the container's rim, cut through it. Screw the base to a half-round bracket as before.

10 Hanging mesh feeders are available from most pet and garden supply stores. Measure the width and length of your feeder and add ¾ in. to both. Set out these dimensions on the board. Use a small container to draw around for the curved ends. Drill a hole in the waste area, and score around the line at the curved ends. Insert the jigsaw blade through the hole and cut along the waste side of the line.

11 Seedcakes and sticks, fruit, and other tidbits can be hung on the board, either to the face or hanging within in a cutout as for the feeder. Use round-headed brass screws for tying the food on.

12 Cut the perches to length from ½ in. diameter dowel, but choose a drill size to ensure a tight fit when the dowel is inserted. Set out the center points and drill the dowel holes either cutting from both sides in turn or into waste material, to prevent the plywood breaking out on the rear face.

SCALES

THIS UNUSUAL BIRD FEEDER DESIGN FEATURES TWO LARGE-DIAMETER DISHES THAT CAN EITHER BOTH BE USED FOR FOOD OR ONE FOR FOOD WHILE THE OTHER CARRIES AN INNER DISH FILLED WITH WATER AS A BIRDBATH. THE HANGING CHAINS WILL DETER LARGE BIRDS FROM USING THE FEEDER AND FRIGHTENING AWAY SMALLER SPECIES. FURTHER RESTRICTION CAN BE INTRODUCED BY NEATLY LINKING HORIZONTAL CHAINS OR THICK CORD BETWEEN THE VERTICAL CHAINS TO FORM A LARGE MESH. REGULARLY CHANGE THE WATER AND CLEAN THE FOOD DISH, REPLACING ANY LEFTOVER FOOD WITH FRESH.

MATERIALS

1 piece of 96 x 2¼ x ¾ in. timber

1 piece of 24 x 8 x 1 in. timber (base)

1 piece of 36 x 1⅜ x ¾ in. timber

1 piece of 36 x 4 x ¾ in. timber

1 piece of 3 x 3 x 9 in. timber (for turning finial and cap)

10 ft. of ⅜ in. link chain (brass or stainless steel)

2 x ¾ in. brass or S/S shackles (or stiff wire for making your own)

2 1 ½ x ³⁄₁₆ in. nuts and bolts (brass or S/S)

6 brass or S/S "S" hooks

2 dishes around 13 in. diameter

1 Cut a length of 2¼ x ¾ in. wood into lengths of 5, 23, 34, and 34 in.

2 Glue the two shorter pieces between the two longer ones, leaving the exact size of sockets for the beam and pan support, and clamp until dry.

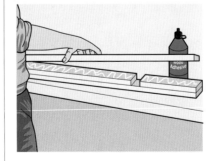

3 Plane the sides of the pillar square. From the base and beam socket, mark out the length of the side moldings.

4 Using an electric router fitted with a self-guiding "ovolo" router bit, cut along each edge in turn; then cut each edge, running the router on the adjacent face. This is to cut

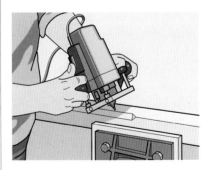

the same detail at the end of the molding on both faces. To do this, the router bit must be set accurately, so do cut several test pieces on waste material to insure that it is correct. Alternatively, a 45-deg. chamfer can be cut with a spokeshave.

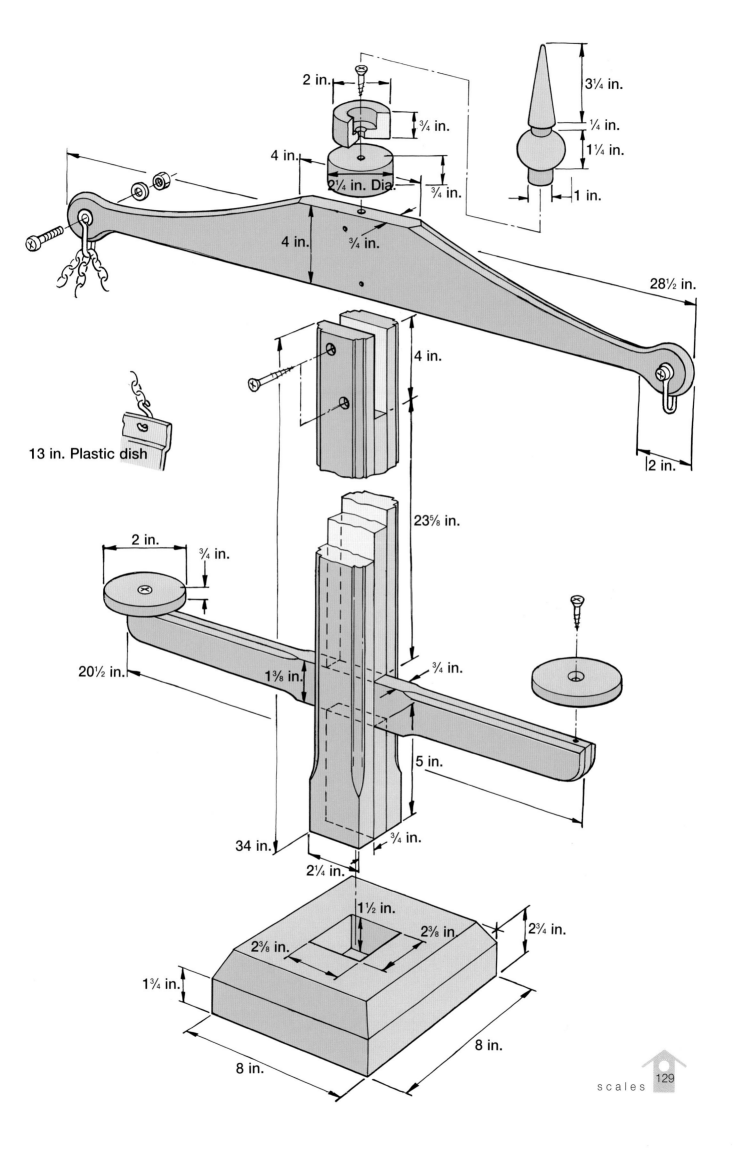

2 in.

¾ in.

4 in.

2¼ in. Dia.

¾ in.

3¼ in.

¼ in.

1¼ in.

1 in.

4 in.

¾ in.

28½ in.

2 in.

4 in.

23⅝ in.

13 in. Plastic dish

2 in.

¾ in.

20½ in.

1⅜ in.

¾ in.

5 in.

34 in.

¾ in.

2¼ in.

1½ in.

2⅜ in

2¾ in.

2⅜ in.

1¾ in.

8 in.

8 in.

5 Draw the beam shape on 4 x ¾ in. piece, and cut it out as accurately as possible with a jigsaw. Plane and sand the edges straight and square.

6 Cut a chamfer around the edges of the beam using either a spokeshave or the electric router fitted with a self-guiding, 45-deg. chamfer router bit.

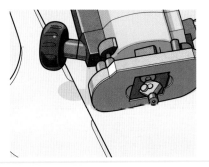

7 Glue the beam in the socket and secure with two screws.

8 Cut the lower pan support from a piece of 1⅜ x ¾ in. wood and chamfer the edges as before. Glue the support in the socket and secure with two screws. At the end of each arm, screw a 2 in. diameter wooden pad.

9 The base is made up of three 8 x 8 x 1 in. pieces. Alternate the grain direction and glue and clamp the blocks until dry. Plane a 45-deg. chamfer along each edge.

10 The pillar is fitted into a mortise cut in the center of the base. Mark out the size of the mortise, equal to the finished size of the pillar. Drill several large-diameter holes to remove most of the waste before squaring the mortise with a chisel. Glue the pillar into the mortise and secure with a screw from beneath.

FINIALS

11 Turn the top finial on a lathe, leaving a ¼ x 1 in. diameter spigot for gluing into the cap. Turn the cap on the lathe or cut it square, leaving a 1 in. diameter socket in the center. Glue and screw the cap onto the top of the pillar and glue the finial into it. Alternatively, use a turned wooden door knob you've bought from the hardware store.

12 Fill any defects and recessed screw heads with epoxy filler and sand all surfaces. Finish the wood with a water-based stain or varnish.

13 Drill through the rim of two 13 in. diameter plastic dishes to take three equally spaced S-hooks. Position the dishes on the pads and measure the length of the chains to the beam, leaving a couple of extra links. Bend a stiff piece of brass or galvanized wire to form a shackle for the chains, fitting the chains before bending the second eye. Drill through the center of the beam ends and bolt through the shackles. Adjust the length of the chains by removing spare links as necessary. Drill one hole through the bottom of the dish and use a small round-headed screw to fasten it to the pad. Drainage holes can be drilled in the bottom of the dishes to stop them filling with rain. For use as a bird bath, use a third dish placed on one of the fixed dishes.

FINISHING TOUCHES

The scales can be mounted on a brick pier of similar dimensions to the base or larger, fitting a capping stone between the two. To secure it, screw two or more long wood screws partway into the underside of the base, and set them into mortar-filled joints or holes in the pier.

PAGODA

AN EASTERN FLAVOR IS INTRODUCED BY THIS COVERED BIRD TABLE WITH ITS CURVED ROOF SUPPORTED ON ROUND PILLARS. SET OFF AMONG PLANTS WITH A TROPICAL FEEL, ITS SCULPTURAL APPEAL IS BOTH ATTRACTIVE AND PRACTICAL, PROVIDING SHELTERED FEEDING FOR SMALLER BIRDS, SUCH AS CHICKADEES, WRENS, AND SPARROWS, WHILE THE OVERHANGING ROOF WILL DETER LARGER, SOMETIMES AGGRESSIVE SPECIES.

MATERIALS

1 piece of 30 x 18 x ½ in. plywood

1 piece of 16 x 16 x ⅜ in. plywood

1 piece of 16 x 10½ x ⅛ in. plywood

1 piece of 16 x 1½ in. diameter dowel

1 piece of 50 x ⅝ in. diameter dowel

1 piece of 22 x 1¼ x ⅜ in. timber

1 piece of ½ in. half-round bead

Exterior wood glue

Screws

Stain and paint

¾ in. molding pins

OTHER TOOLS

Pair of compasses or a beam compass
(see page 121 for beam compass)

ROOF

1 Draw out one of the roof ends on ⅜ in. plywood, setting out the curve to a radius of 6½ in. Score across the grain and along the curved lines before cutting. From the first, mark out and cut the second end. Clamp the two together and finish the edges square, using a plane for the straight edges and a rasp and/or abrasive paper over a curved sanding block for the curved edges.

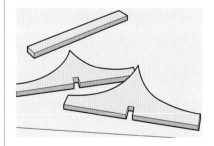

2 Cut two 10¾ x 15½ in. roof panels from ⅛ in. plywood and plane the edges straight and square. Measure 1¼ in. in from both ends and draw a line parallel to the short edges on both panels.

3 Clamp an end piece in the vise and run a ribbon of glue along one of the curved edges of one end piece. Bend one of the panels against the bench edge, and hold the curve with a string tourniquet or webbing clamp. Align the end piece with the line drawn on the panel and pin it along the curved surface. Apply glue to the other end piece, and pin this in place in the same way. When dry, repeat this procedure with the other panel.

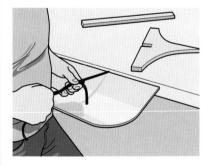

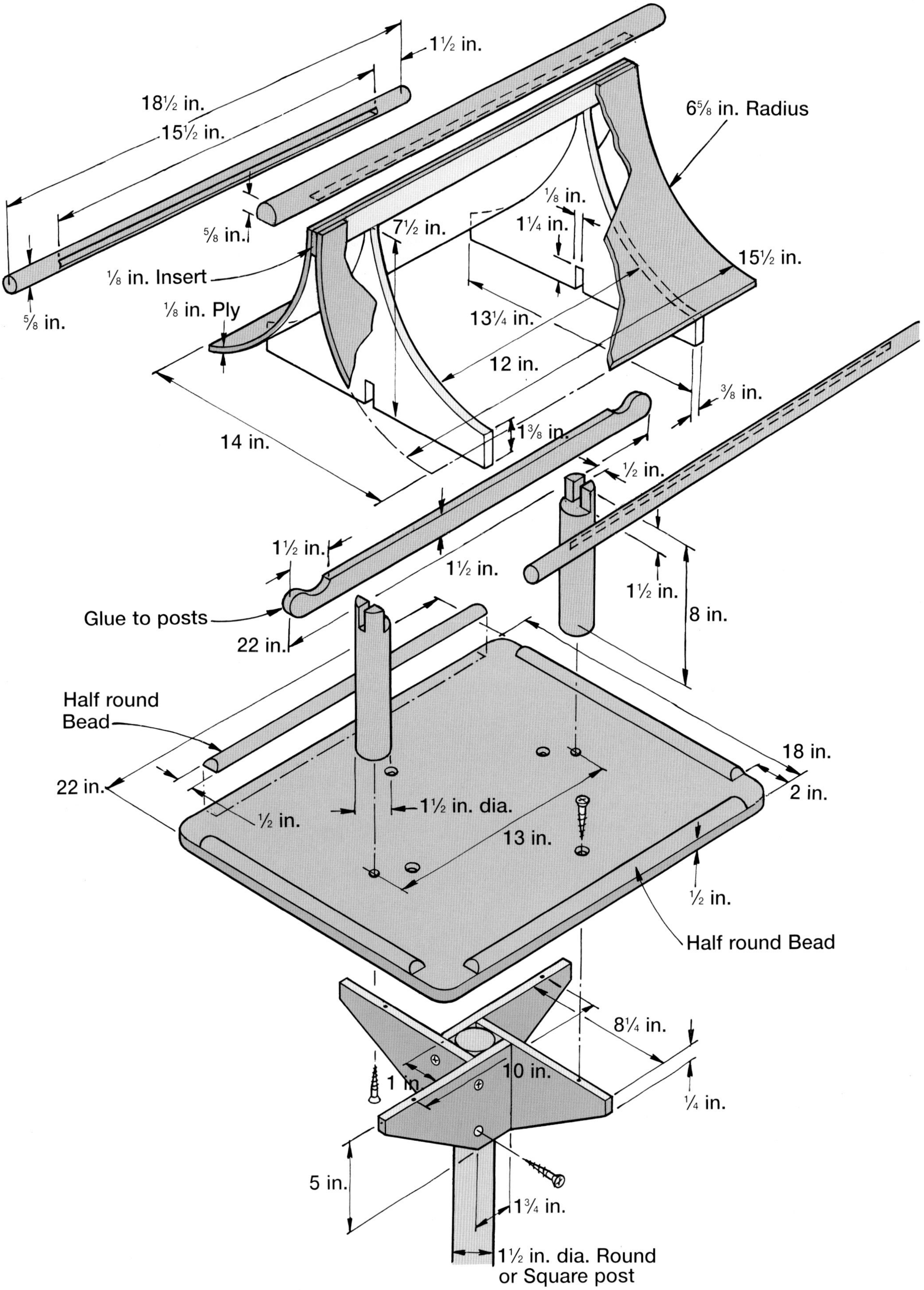
1½ in.
18½ in.
15½ in.
6⅝ in. Radius
⅛ in.
⅝ in.
7½ in.
1¼ in.
⅛ in. Insert
15½ in.
⅝ in.
⅛ in. Ply
13¼ in.
12 in.
⅜ in.
1⅜ in.
14 in.
½ in.
1½ in.
1½ in.
1½ in.
Glue to posts
8 in.
22 in.
Half round
Bead
18 in.
22 in.
2 in.
½ in.
1½ in. dia.
13 in.
½ in.
Half round Bead
8¼ in.
10 in.
1 in.
¼ in.
5 in.
1¾ in.
1½ in. dia. Round
or Square post

Jig for grooving dowel using an electric router

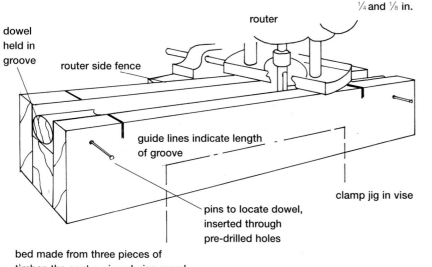

cutter diameters
¼ and ⅛ in.

router

dowel held in groove

router side fence

guide lines indicate length of groove

clamp jig in vise

pins to locate dowel, inserted through pre-drilled holes

bed made from three pieces of timber, the center piece being equal in width to the dowel diameter

4 Cut three 18½ in. lengths of ⅝ in. dowel. Along the length of one piece cut a ¼ in. groove, stopping 1½ in. from each end. This is most easily done by pinning the dowel into a grooved batten and running a router, fitted with a ¼ in. diameter cutter along it. Square the ends of the groove with a chisel and glue the dowel over the top edges of the curved panels. Repeat this with the bottom edges but using a ⅛ in. diameter router cutter.

SUPPORT RAIL AND COLUMNS

5 Cut two 8 in. lengths of 1½ in. dowel and cut a 1½ in. long halving, half the diameter of the dowel wide. At 90 deg. to the face of the halving, cut a ½ in. groove to the same length. In the bottom of each dowel, drill a ³⁄₁₆ in. pilot hole.

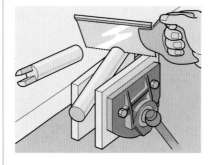

6 Cut a 22 x 1½ x ½ in. long batten, round the two ends, and cut a semicircular notch of similar diameter (i.e. 1½ in.). Glue and pin the roof onto the two dowel posts.

BASEBOARD AND MOUNTING BRACKET

7 Cut the 18 x 22 in. baseboard from ½ in. plywood and plane the edges straight and square.

8 Cut two 13 and two 14 in. lengths of ½ in. half-round bead and chamfer all eight ends. Glue and pin the beads to the top face of the baseboard.

9 Draw around a coin to mark the radiused corners. Score around the line before cutting with a jigsaw and sanding to a smooth curve.

10 Mark out and cut the four support brackets from ¾ in. wood. Screw the four pieces together and position them on the underside of the baseboard. Drill through the baseboard and glue and screw the battens to the underside.

11 After filling any defects and recessed pin and screw heads with epoxy filler, sand all surfaces smooth. Paint the roof with exterior masonry paint.

12 Paint both the base board and pillars with a suitable non-toxic, exterior-grade varnish or stain.

N A T U R A L

B R A N C H

A BRANCH FROM A DEAD OR FELLED TREE CAN BE USED TO FORM AN ATTRACTIVE FEEDING STATION, PARTICULARLY ON HARD-SURFACED YARDS, BALCONIES, AND PATIOS, SELECT A FALLEN BRANCH THAT HAS A PLEASING AND BALANCED SHAPE, PREFERABLY WITH A SOUND AND ATTRACTIVELY TEXTURED BARK.

MATERIALS

Selected branch
Proprietary nut feeder

OTHER TOOLS

Logging saw
Flat or spade bits

1 Carefully select a suitably shaped branch and cut off any broken, unsightly or uneven side shoots. Leave the bark on if it is securely attached.

2 Cut any small branches or shoots close to the main branch. These can be used for hanging tidbits such as bunches of bacon rind or seedcakes. A store-bought mesh feeder can be hung in this way. Orange and apple halves should be secured by spearing them over shoots or dowels inserted into drilled holes in the branch. Avoid nails and metal spikes as these may present a danger to the birds, especially if they rust away leaving sharp or jagged points.

3 Natural cracks and pockets not only harbor grubs and insects naturally, but can be filled with seed or other bird food.

4 Pockets can also be cut using a spade or flat bit to drill into the branch. Vary the diameter and

depth of the holes to create a feature. It may also be possible to encourage small birds to nest in a large hole but, if you do try this, do not continue to encourage other birds to feed in such close proximity by putting out food and water.

5 Small containers of food or water can be held in loops of twisted wire pushed into small holes drilled in the branch.

FINISHING

6 Ensure that the branch is securely mounted, ideally resting against a wall or corner formed by two walls or fences. Use a galvanized metal strap to secure it to the brickwork or wooden posts.

7 The base of the branch should be cut to stand flat. Alternatively stand it in a wooden tub or ceramic or terracotta planter filled with pea gravel or larger stones.

CLOCK TOWER

THIS CLOCKTOWER BIRD TABLE WILL PROVIDE THE IDEAL FOCAL POINT IN ANY SMALL YARD OR GARDEN, JUST AS ITS LARGER COUNTERPART DID IN SMALL TOWNS OF OLD. FITTED WITH A QUARTZ CLOCK MOVEMENT, IT HAS A PRACTICAL FUNCTION AS WELL AS PROVIDING SHELTERED FEEDING FOR A WIDE VARIETY OF BIRDS IN TIMES OF BAD WEATHER. ALTERNATIVELY, THE CLOCK TOWER CAN BE CONVERTED INTO A NESTING BOX, BUT DO REMEMBER NOT TO PUT FOOD OUT ON THE TABLE IF YOUNG BIRDS ARE ON THE NEST.

MATERIALS

1 piece of 24 x 18 x ½ in. plywood

1 piece of 24 x 1¼ x 1¼ in. timber

1 piece of 48 x 48 x ⅜ in. plywood

1 piece of 48 x 1 in. half-round bead

1 piece of 8 x ⅝ x 1 in. timber

1 piece of 36 x 3⅛ x ¾ in. timber

Exterior wood glue

Screws

Stain and paint

¾ in. molding pins

4½ in. square of clear perspex

4½ in. square of white laminate

Quartz clock movement

OTHER TOOLS

³⁄₁₆ in. dowel bit

Beam compass

ROOF

1 Draw the four triangular roof segments (base 16 in. x height 12½ in.) on a piece of ⅜ in. plywood with the grain running along their length and the wide and narrow ends alternated. Leave a gap of ⅛ in. between each to allow for the width of the saw blade. Score across the grain along the angled edges before cutting.

2 Cut out each segment and mark one face of each (this will be the inside face when the segments are glued together). Stack all four segments together in a vise, and plane all to the same size with all the edges square.

3 On the opposite edges of two of the segments mark an angle of 60 deg. and join the lower points with a line drawn parallel to the edge. The actual finished angle will be slightly greater, but this will provide a good guide to work to.

4 Bevel the edges of the two segments by planing down to the line, taking care not to decrease the width of each piece. Check and adjust the angle by lightly planing until their faces mate along their full length when their bases are set at an angle of 90 deg. Set a bevel gauge to the finished edge angle and mark and plane the remaining segment edges to this angle.

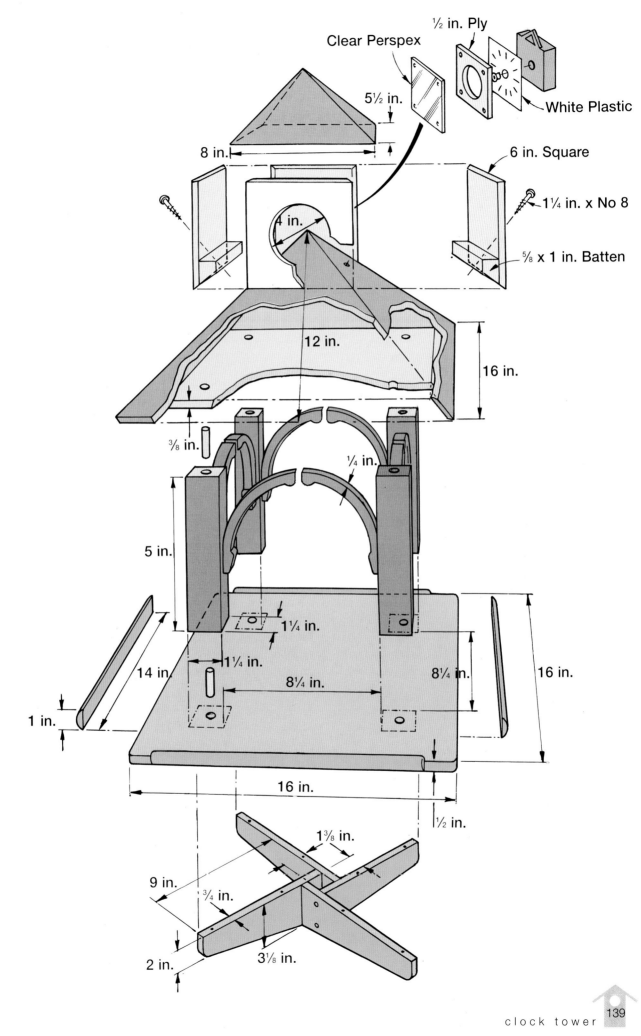

Clear Perspex

½ in. Ply

White Plastic

5½ in.

8 in.

6 in. Square

1¼ in. x No 8

4 in.

⅝ x 1 in. Batten

12 in.

16 in.

⅜ in.

¼ in.

5 in.

1¼ in.

1¼ in.

14 in

8¼ in.

8¼ in.

16 in.

1 in.

16 in.

½ in.

1⅜ in.

9 in.

¾ in.

2 in.

3⅛ in.

5 Glue and pin the four segments together. To hold the roof square while drying, pin two battens at 90 deg. onto a piece of waste board and push the roof against them. Pin two further battens against the remaining two edges and pin these securely.

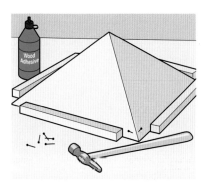

6 Cut a square panel of ⅜ in. plywood to fit into the underside of the roof ⅜ in. above the bottom edge. Draw lines parallel to and ⅜ in. in from each edge on one face of the panel. Plane down to the line to leave an angle of 45 deg. around the edge. Glue and pin the panel into the base of the roof.

7 When completely dry, plane or sand the bottom edges straight and square and finish the vertical joints of the roof flush.

PILLARS

8 Cut four 1¼ x 1¼ x 5 in. pillars. Drill a hole centrally in one end of each to take a ³⁄₁₆ in. dowel.

9 On the underside of the roof, mark out the position of the pillars – leaving a dimension of 8¼ in. between each – and mark the center point of each pillar. Drill a ³⁄₁₆ in. hole at each point to take the dowels. Apply glue to the top of the pillar and the dowels and glue the pillars in place, square to the baseboard sides, using masking tape to hold them in place and square until dry.

BRACKETS

10 Draw out the shape of one bracket on a piece of ⅜ in. plywood. Score the curved lines and cut the bracket out. Smooth the edges with a file and/or abrasive paper.

11 Use the first bracket as a template for drawing the seven remaining ones. Cut and finish all the brackets and drill a fine pilot hole to take the fixing pins. Glue and pin each bracket to the pillars and roof.

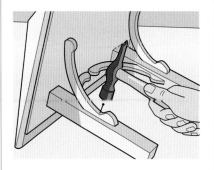

CLOCKTOWER

12 Cut four 8 x 5½ in. triangular segments from ⅜ in. plywood and make up the small roof in a similar fashion to the main roof, planing the joint face angles, but omitting the square panel.

13 Cut four 6 in. square ⅜ in. plywood side pieces and mark the inside face. Plane a 45 deg. miter along two opposite edges on the marked face of each. Plane a 60 deg. angle on the opposite faces of the other two edges.

14 Use a pair of compasses to mark out a 4 in. circle in the center of one panel. With a router or jigsaw, cut out the circle, finishing the edges with abrasive paper wrapped over a curved block.

15 Glue and pin the four sides together and check for squareness. Glue and pin the roof to the mitered edge of the walls.

16 Cut an 8 in. length of ⅝ x 1 in. batten and plane one face to an angle of 45 deg. Cut the batten into two pieces and glue them to the inside bottom edges of two opposite sides, the beveled face being flush to the beveled face of the batten.

17 Drill neat countersunk holes through the side panels and battens to take 1¼ in. x 8 gauge brass screws. Stand the clocktower on the roof and drill pilot holes to position the holding-down screws.

18 Quartz clock movements and hands can be bought quite inexpensively from most craft supplies outlets. Cut a 4½ x 4½ in. square of white plastic and drill the center to take the threaded tube of the movement. Set out the clock face on this piece using black acrylic paint or self-adhesive numbers. Cut a 4½ x 4½ in. square of clear perspex or other transparent sheet.

19 Mark out a 4½ x 4½ in. square of ½ in. plywood and draw a 4 in. circle in the center. In the center of the square cut a 4 in. diameter circle as before. Cut out the square and clamp all three pieces in a vise, lining up their edges. Drill a ¹⁄₁₆ in. diameter circle in each corner, through all three pieces. Use these holes to mount the movement, using ⅜ in. round-headed brass screws. (Fit the battery and set the clock to the correct time before mounting the clock housing to the main roof, when the finished bird table is positioned outdoors.)

20 After filling any defects and pin holes (do not fill over the heads of the two mounting screws), sand all surfaces smooth. Paint the roof and walls with exterior masonry paint.

BASEBOARD AND MOUNTING BRACKET

21 Cut the 16 x 16 in. baseboard from ½ in. plywood and plane the edges straight and square.

22 Cut four 14 x 14 in. lengths of 1 in. half-round bead, plane a narrow flat along the edges and round the ends. Glue and pin the beads to the edge of the baseboard.

23 Draw around a coin to mark the radiused corners. Score around the line before cutting with a jigsaw and sanding to a smooth curve.

24 Mark out and cut the four support brackets from a piece of ¾ in. wood. Screw the four pieces together and position them on the underside of the baseboard. Drill through the baseboard and glue and screw the battens to the underside.

FINISHING

After filling any defects and recessed pin and screw heads with epoxy filler, sand all surfaces smooth. Paint the roof with exterior masonry paint.

Paint both the baseboard and pillars with a suitable non-toxic, exterior-grade varnish or stain.

Further Reading

The Complete Birdhouse Book, Donald and Lillian
Stokes, Stokes Nature Guides. Little, Brown and
Company, Boston
Birdscaping Your Garden, George Adams,
Lansdowne Publishing Pty Ltd, Sydney
The Bird Table Book, Tony Soper,
David & Charles, Newton Abbot
Nest Boxes, by Chris du Feu. *BTO Guide 23.*
BTO, National Centre for Ornithology, Norfolk

Basic Woodworking Techniques, Dick Burrows,
Apple Press, London
Collins Pocket Guide to Birds of Britain and Europe
H. Heinzel, R. F. Fitter, J. Parslow, Collins, London
A Field Guide to the Birds of Australia, Graham Pizzey,
Collins, Sydney
Peterson Field Guides, Western Birds, Eastern Birds,
Roger Tory Peterson, Houghton Mifflin

RECOMMENDED DIMENSIONS FOR BIRDHOUSE ENTRANCES

Bird	Entrance Hole	Bird	Entrance Hole
Bluebirds	1½ in.	Owls	2½–4 up to 6 in.
Blue Tits	1 in.	Pardalotes	1–1½ in.
Chickadees	1½ in.	Purple Martin	2–2½ in.
Ducks	3½–4½ in.	Robins	1½ in.
Finches	1½–2 in.	Rosellas	3–4 in.
Flycatchers	1½–2½ in.	Sparrows	1¼–2 in.
Galahs	4¾ in.	Swallows	1 x 2½ in.
Lorikeets	2½ in.	Titmice	1⅜–1½ in.
Kookaburas	5 in.	Woodpeckers	1¼–2 in.
Nuthatches	1½ in.	Wrens	1¼–1½ in.

Acknowledgments

The Pubisher wishes to thank all those who helped in the compilation of this book. They are

James R. Hill, III
Purple Martin Conservation Association
Edinboro University of Pennsylvania
Edinboro, PA 16444, USA

Royal Australasian Ornithologists Union
415 Riversdale Road
Hawthorn East,
Vic 3123, Australia

University Botanic Garden, Cambridge, England
Camas UK Ltd of Exeter, England

Lieutenant Colonel and Mrs Bryan Barrett
Sue and Gerry Feakes
Jo and Brian Montandon
Peter Bates of Brampton Garden Centre
Brampton Park Golf Club Ltd.
Gibbs and Dandy
all in and around Huntingdon, England

Anna Parker
Jack Padfield of Centenary Towers,
*whose beautifully designed gothic bird tables
pictured on page 6 are available for purchase
from*
Designs and Installations,
11 Romilly Road
London N4 2QZ, England

PICTURE CREDITS
p. 6 top & 9 Wayne Lankinen,
Aquila Photographics
p. 6 bottom Andrew Lawson, Centenary Towers
p. 7 Glenturret Distillery Ltd, Crieff, Perthshire
p. 8 & 15 J. Feltwell, Wildlife Matters
p. 10 M. Collins, Garden Matters
p. 12 Mike Wilkes, Aquila Photographics
p. 13 & 15 James R. Hill, III

INDEX